CLUELESS GRINGOS IN PARADISE

ADVENTURES WITH MY HUSBAND, HIS PTSD, AND TWO ENORMOUS SERVICE DOGS

ALSO BY
PAMELA FOSTER

SOLDIER'S HEART

NOISY CREEK

BIGFOOT BLUES

BIGFOOT MAMAS

CLUELESS GRINGOS IN PARADISE

ADVENTURES WITH MY HUSBAND, HIS PTSD, AND TWO ENORMOUS SERVICE DOGS

PAMELA FOSTER

MEATH
PRESS

an imprint of
ARBROATH ABBEY PRESS

OGHMA

CREATIVE MEDIA

Bentonville, Arkansas • Los Angeles, California

www.oghmacreative.com

Library of Congress Cataloging-in-Publication Data

Names: Foster, Pamela, author.
Title: Clueless Gringos in Paradise/Pamela Foster.
Description: Second Edition. | Bentonville: Meath, 2020.
Identifiers: LCCN: 2019937261 | ISBN: 978-1-63373-503-3 (hardcover) |
ISBN: 978-1-63373-504-0 (trade paperback) | ISBN: 978-1-63373-505-7 (eBook)
Subjects: | BISAC: HUMOR/Topic/Men, Women & Relationships |
HUMOR/Topic/Travel « BIOGRAPHY & AUTOBIOGRAPHY/Women |
TRAVEL/Central America | BIOGRAPHY & AUTOBIOGRAPHY/People with Disabilities
LC record available at: https://lccn.loc.gov/2019937261

Meath Press hardcover edition January, 2020

Jacket Design by Casey W. Cowan
Interior Design by Erin Ladd
Editing by Cyndy Prasse Miller & Chelsea Cambeis

Nonfiction books from Arbroath Abbey Press may be purchased for educational, business, or sales and promotional use. For information, please contact our General Administration Department at the following email address: venessa@oghmacreative.com.

Published by Meath Press, an imprint of Arbroath Abbey Press, a subsidiary of The Oghma Book Group.

This one is for Jack, my biggest hero and greatest challenge.
And for Mona, because she saved the emails.

PROLOGUE
THE BOULDER FROM HELL

YOU KNOW THAT guy in Utah, Aron Ralston? The one that went hiking around Moab and ended up trapped by the boulder from Hell and had to hack off his hand at the wrist with a pocket knife? I'm beginning to think of that tragic tale as a near perfect analogy for marriage.

I mean, think about the way it probably went. The guy works like a fool just to get himself to this glorious, starkly beautiful environment of lurking death. He be-bops along, enjoys the rose-tinged boulders, thinks he's the luckiest, cleverest fool in the history of the world to have discovered these deep clefts and smooth surfaces.

Next thing he knows, he jumps down into this inviting crevasse and looks up just in time to see this bitch of a boulder falling through the air to pin his wrist to the side of the mother of all rocks. You know he's gotta be watching that stone prison falling toward him in slow motion, like an innocently-smiling virgin stepping inexorably down the aisle, and part of his brain has got to be screaming, "N-o-o-o!"

And the boulder. Let's think about that for a minute. Birthed by the bedrock, prepared for eons by rain and wind and the natural erosion of the mother rock to fall with no more thought than, well, than a bride going to her goofily-smiling groom. Slipping, as easily as nature herself, through the golden, red-tinged air, to fall precisely, pinning the hapless young man to the side of the canyon he thought to plunge into with the reckless joy of ignorant youth.

Okay.

So he's pinned.

He spends a day or two trying to think his way out of his predicament. He denies he's stuck. He wiggles and squirms and stretches and moans. He enjoys a sunset or two. Prays to the God that created the freaking boulder. Watches a couple of killer sunrises. Decides to cut off his hand to save the rest of his life.

If you've ever been married, go ahead, tell me you've never been right there.

But, nuh-uh, nope. That hand's not coming off that easily. His tiny little pocket knife is not going to cut through the solid bone of the good wrist given to him by a loving Lord.

So he waits. He gives up. He resigns himself to living the rest of his short, miserable life trapped by this rosy stone to the side of the bedrock. He waits. If he'd had a TV, he'd have watched it, remote clutched firmly in his good hand, proof of his amazing control over his life.

He thinks about all the people he knows who seem to skip merrily through their little jaunts in the countryside. He wonders what the hell is the matter with him that he didn't just leap over the abyss and keep enjoying his sunny freedom.

He remembers the life he had before he trapped himself in the wilderness. So long ago now, it feels like it happened to someone else. Someone happy. Someone free.

Maybe he thinks about his mother and the lies she told him about the joys to be found in committing to that leap of faith. He waits. He drinks his own urine. Watches the fuzzy black images of the circling buzzards.

He waits. He thinks about what he'd do with the rest of his life if he could just get out of this mess. He drifts for a while in a haze of pre-death exhaustion. He thinks about those dark, feathered portents of rot and decay circling silently, lazily, patiently over his head, drawn by the smell of the gangrene. He smiles. He waits just a little longer, letting his hope build his strength and courage.

Then he plunges his tiny steel blade into the now-rotten flesh of his wrist. Even now, nothing is quick or easy. He cuts and scrapes and digs for the joint. He screams and rants and gives up a dozen times. Only his sure knowledge that he will die if he can't escape keeps him hacking away at his stinking flesh.

In the end, he's free. Missing a part of himself, half-dead from the ordeal, but free. And still miles from safety or any solid hope of survival. Now he puts one foot in front of the other, prays he's lucid enough that he's navigating in the correct direction, and just keeps walking. For many, many steps, long past the time when common sense dictates he give up, curl peacefully in a fetal position, and embrace his death, he walks. One painful step at a time. Not letting himself think about the reality that he's hacked off a vital piece of his own body. He just staggers toward what he hopes is the direction of life.

Having done all he can to save himself, it's a combination of luck and love that save him. Other hikers, strolling blissfully along on their own adventure, stumble across him—very nearly dead on his feet, though still standing. At the same time, his mother, frantic for days now at his disappearance, has begged, prodded, and threatened the authorities into putting a helicopter in the air to look for him. That helicopter is less than a mile away when he's discovered by the happy family of hikers.

At the hospital, the experts bring him back from the dead. Then they cut off his arm again. Higher up and cleaner. They rig him up with an artificial hand. He even has a prosthetic with a climbing hook. Unbelievably, he soon convinces himself he's come out of his ordeal better than new. He gets on with his life with a fresh joy in each new dawn. He rushes right out and looks for another virgin wilderness to explore and enjoy. After all, he's better prepared this time. Why, he even has a steel hook to replace the soft, vulnerable, puny hand he had during his first ordeal.

Admittedly, I might be having a bad day. But seriously, isn't that whole trapped-in-the-desert-drink-your-own-urine ordeal a perfect analogy for marriage? That platitude that everyone tells you when you're going through a rough spot in your marital life? You know the one.

"What doesn't kill you makes you stronger."

Bullshit.

Life can be hard enough that it leaves you crippled and panting on the side of a forsaken road, just praying for the rot to set in so you can scrape, hack, and saw your way out of yet another disaster, leaving an additional appendage to feed the earth from which you've managed to drag your sorry ass.

I told you I was having a bad day.

Here's why.

ONE
ONE GIANT STEP OVER THE LINE

MY HUSBAND, JACK, and I sit in our old-people recliners— you know, the ones you see on TV with old people in them— and watch CNN while we pet the fur-covered, 150-pound trunkless elephants we call dogs, and contemplate another winter in the high desert of Arizona.

"You know what?" I ask rhetorically.

Jack doesn't answer. We've been married long enough that, first of all, he knows one of my lead-ins to a discussion about our lives when he hears it, and secondly, he's trained his brain to simply filter out nine-tenths of what comes floating out of my mouth.

Knowing this, with no encouragement whatsoever, I continue, "It feels like we're just sitting here waiting to die."

He turns his head and looks at me.

A minute later, he says, "Yeah. It does, doesn't it?"

After breakfast, I say, "Let's move to someplace green and warm with a beautiful blue ocean."

This, right here, turns out to be the equivalent of saying, "I'll bet we could strap these two giant dogs to our backs and just leap right across that rocky abyss over yonder. Don't worry about those loose boulders. We'll be fine."

By noon, I've surfed the web and found Bocas del Toro in the Republic of Panama—a thousand tiny islands in the southern Caribbean, right across the border from Costa Rica. A paradise of palm trees, pale cerulean blue water, and monkeys. Too close to the equator for hurricanes. Plus, every website assures me they speak English. Our new home?

By early afternoon, Jack has called the realtor and set up an appointment for her to come out to our adobe brick house and five prickly desert acres. Does this seem a rash and inappropriate, some might even say insane, response to you? Ah well, then I'm betting you've never lived with a combat veteran, someone for whom every hour since returning from battle has been dull and gray and boring. Someone who carries the horror and thrill of war within themselves and keeps it smashed down deep and covered only by emotional deadening or maybe with booze or pills. Someone who followed a flag into an unwinnable war and replaced youthful innocence with a shiny medal. Someone who, since returning physically from battle, uproots his life on a regular basis in the hope of catching a single glimpse of the adrenaline rush he was issued as a seventeen-year-old Marine, along with a pair of jungle boots and an M14—the power to be God.

If you live with one of these warriors, you already know we keep researching Panama. We keep walking toward the dream of a life that sparkles and shines and pours adrenaline, like good booze, into the bloodstream.

Everything we find on the internet about the little isthmus of a country looks good. It's affordable. The political situation is stable. Noriega's in jail in Florida. Right? The government has set up a variety of appealing incentives to encourage immigration and investment. The islands of Bocas look beautiful—white sand beaches and clear blue water. The place looks like heaven. And every single webpage and blog insists the people speak both Spanish and English, promising an entire country of educated bilinguals eager to work for you where the average income is under $200 a month. Domestic help within reach!

We lived on the Caribbean coast of Mexico for six years in a trailer set up in a tiny beach community called Paamul. *Gringos, all gringos* there. Lots of Texan spoken, but only Spanish outside the community. I spoke kitchen Spanish. Not much more. Meaning I could order in a restaurant, but only the most patient local would follow me through a maze of broken Spanish to go much beyond *I'd like ice with my Coke, please.* Of course, Panama has had a huge community of Americans for years because of the canal. So maybe they learned English while our forefathers were fighting off yellow fever, building and then managing the waterway for a hundred years. Yeah, that makes sense. That must be how an entire, albeit tiny, Central American country became bilingual. The internet wouldn't lie. Right?

Okay. So, a week later, the house is on the market, and we're booked on a reconnaissance flight to Panama for the first of November. That's forty-seven days away. I was going to say we were making progress, but in retrospect, moving toward our chosen goal is probably closer to the truth.

You need to know about these dogs we have, these Italian Mastiffs or Cane Corsos. Chesty and Rocca. But before I can tell you about the dogs, I have to fill you in on a little information about my husband.

As I mentioned, Jack is a former Marine. He served in Vietnam "in-country" when there was a lot of shooting. Who the hell he or any other military personnel were actually serving over there is still up for debate. The point is, our government sent him, and in all ignorance and patriotism and innocence, he went. Into the quagmire. Six months in-country, he disarmed a landmine the Marine Corps way. Put his fingers in his ears and stepped softly with the toe of his combat boot. Or, so he tells it. At any rate, he died, and given the place he was leaving at that moment, he was happy to go. Except the damn corpsman dragged him out of the nice, warm, peaceful light and slammed him back into the pain and stink of the jungle.

So it's thirty years later and, except for the constant pain and raging Post-traumatic Stress Disorder (PTSD), he's pretty much gotten over the whole war experience thing. He's still pissed at the corpsman, but he's managed to live with it, and except for the five previous wives and the changing jobs every few years, he's doing just fine, thank you, nothing wrong with him. There's not much to be done with the physical pain, but one of the ways he deals with his PTSD is by having service dogs. Another way he handles the residue of the trauma is to make chronically-impulsive, life-changing decisions based on nothing more than an overriding sense of boredom. But you have, perhaps, already caught on to this.

The dogs are trained to let him know when someone is coming up behind him, to cover his back when he's in public, to distract him when he gets anxious, and to reassure him when he's nervous. It works slick. We haven't had to flee a grocery store, leaving a full cart of food, since he got the first dog. We even go to movies now. And restaurants. Of course, he still sits with his back to the wall, and he persists in believing that the name of Ted Turner's ex-wife is Jane Fucking Fonda, but really, he's pretty much recovered from the whole war trauma thing.

Okay. So, back to the dogs. Chesty—after WWII Lieutenant General Lewis Burwell "Chesty" Puller—and Rocca—after her world champion weight pull and doggie triathlon winning daddy, Rocco. We got the male first, and the Veteran's Administration sent my husband to school in Hutto, Texas to learn to train the dog to assist specifically with Jack's disabilities. Because part of the dog's job is to give Jack a sense of safety in public places, Chesty is big. He weighs just over 110 pounds. That's a lot of dog to take everywhere with you, so Chesty had to be trained to behave perfectly. No screwing around here or the whole deal wasn't going to work. It took a lot of time and cussing and patience and fussing and energy to achieve this goal.

Our biggest mistake, I believe, was in naming the dog after a Marine. *The Marine.* At any rate, precisely like a Marine, the dog had to be re-trained every day. Like a Marine, Chesty was the handsomest thing on any block, especially in his red and blue working-dog cape. And, once again like all Marines, he forgot everything he'd ever known the very instant a pretty woman paid any attention to him. Still, eventually, Chesty was ready to begin his working life.

Then, because there is no boundary or line in the sand I can draw that Jack will not casually step over (this is going to become increasingly clear to you as I continue with this story), we got a female pup to train as a backup for Chesty. Making herself comfortable in our home in the desert, our baby girl, Rocca, weighing in at 148 pounds. Fully trained, she is calmer than Chesty and more protective, but not as attuned to Jack's moods. She's also the undisputed boss of our macho Marine-named boy. Except, of course, on those occasions when she has a need for that manly appendage he carries between his legs. Then she's the quintessential Southern belle.

All right, so now you've got the picture a little more clearly. We're bored. We've been in Arizona long enough for the minimalist beauty of the desert to have long ago worn off. We're ready for our next adventure, but on this journey, we'll be traveling with two humongous canine companions.

The house is on the market, the recon flight is booked, and we're entertaining ourselves by reading everything we can get our hands on about the Republic of Panama and visiting all the chat rooms for ex-patriots living in that Central American country. The place continues to sound good.

We're told that the Caribbean island section of the country, Bocas del Toro (translation: Mouths of the Bull) is thirty minutes from a hospital and a Price Smart. So civilization is within easy reach, but far enough away not to encroach too aggressively. We figure we'll get a little panga boat instead of a car to get us between islands and take the local buses once we get to the mainland. When we go out for the day, we'll be able to leave the dogs with the maid or the gardener. Remember those smiling hordes of bilinguals tickled to work for $200 a month? Every *gringo* and rich Panamanian down there has domestic help, according to our research. It's the way of life in Latin America and considered a boon to the local economy. Panama is looking more and more like an undiscovered tropical paradise. Clear blue water, little verdant jungle islands edged in white sand, and most of the comforts of home, too. Plus, they speak English.

Okay, okay, okay. I know. Way too good to be true. But you've gotta remember how bored we are, how desperate to find something with which to entertain ourselves besides looking deep within our souls to discover the peace that surpasses understanding. It's time to move on, and Bocas del Toro looks promising. We'll go and check it out, and if it looks as good as everything we're reading, we'll head on down. If not, well, Jack assures me it's a big world out there.

Here's how that conversation went:

"I don't know, Honey," I say. "I mean, if it were just you and me, then I agree, we could go anywhere. Assuming we can find a buyer for the house. We could just leave the money from the sale in the bank and travel the world and explore. But we have these two giant dogs."

Try to see this with me, the exact condescending tilt of Jack's big white-haired head, the slight cocking of the left eyebrow indicating irritation, the precise tone of voice as though speaking to a not-too-terribly-bright child.

"Why do you have to be negative?" He sighs. "There won't be any problem traveling with the dogs. Trust me."

"But, maybe we should wait to sell the house until we know exactly where we're going."

Yes, I know. It was me who had the bright idea to move in the first place. I'm the one who mentioned greener pastures, where the summers didn't feel like walking into a pizza oven each time I stepped outside. But we seem to be building momentum at an alarming rate. I can almost feel that boulder shifting its position ever so slightly above our heads.

Again, Jack gives me the tone, the head tilt, the cocked eyebrow.

"Stop worrying. Everything will be great. Hasn't it always turned out good for us when you just trusted me?"

And, just like that, I'm remembering the hurricane, and before I can open my mouth, he's read my mind.

"One tiny little mistake, and you're never going to let me forget it!"

TWO

SERENITY IN A HURRICANE

(OR THE HURRICANE AND JACK'S SHRINKING MANHOOD)

W E'VE BEEN MARRIED fifteen years, Jack and I. In that time, we've lived on the Big Island of Hawaii, the Caribbean coast of Mexico, the high desert of Arizona, and traveled the United States in an old motor home. Jack says before he met me, he changed jobs and wives every five years. Now he's retired, and this wife just moves with him to each new location. It's not a lifestyle for everyone, but it works for us, more or less.

You know the Serenity Prayer? "God grant me the serenity to accept the things I cannot change, courage to change the things I can, and wisdom to know the difference?" Well, living with Jack only works if he has the reins firmly in hand. The list of things I can control is thin at best. It makes for a wild and bumpy ride, but I'm never bored. The man would walk through fire for me, but he's never going to acknowledge that it is most often his fingers closed around the smoking match.

One of those things I cannot change.

The hurricane episode happened when we were living on the beach in the Mexican Caribbean, about sixty miles south of Cancun, in the community of Paamul. At that time, Paamul was a small, funky little trailer park where an interesting, slightly shady, and decidedly odd collection of *gringos* rented narrow slots of sand from a local *politico*. We all built wooden decks and shade *palapas* over our trailers. *Palapas* are palm-leafed shelters the local Mayans are happy to build to protect a *gringo's* frog-belly-white skin from the tropical sun for the low, low price of whatever the above-mentioned clueless foreigner is stupid enough to pay.

We dragged a 35-foot park-model trailer the length of Mexico. A trip that still makes me shake and my left eye twitch whenever I think about it. But that's another story. Let's just say we were robbed at gun point, sat on the highway in the blazing sun for three days—halted by a political demonstration which blocked the only road south—while hardy little brown men with large machetes ranted in Spanish what we assumed were the instructions, "Kill all the *gringos* first."

That was the good part of the trip, before the transmission died three times, and we sat in three different dirt yards and visited with the locals while the children chased the geese and turkeys and pigs and chickens to retrieve the small, probably inconsequential parts of our transmission that were scattered about in the freshly swept dirt. I've pretty much recovered from that little adventure, but still, please, give me just a minute. The twitching goes away much quicker now.

Okay. So. We're set up under our termite-infested *palapa* on the eastern Mexico coast, enjoying the pale blue sky and the clear turquoise waters of the Caribbean, when we begin to hear rumors that a class five hurricane is headed our way.

Let's rethink this.

We've built a grass house over a mobile home in a hurricane zone. Huh. Remind me again. What happened to the little pig that built his house of straw? We throw a couple of hurricane parties, talk loud and bold, keep a sharp ear cocked to the weather channel, pack some clothes and a couple bottles of water into the van. We do our best not to hear the wolf calling for us to come on out and play.

Just after midnight on day three, a knock at the aluminum door of the trailer announces the evacuation order. We had a normal-sized dog then, Truffles. The best dog in the whole world. Calm, disciplined, only slightly neurotic, she was a Shar-Pei the color of milk chocolate. So we load Truffles into the car along with a cooler of goldfish. We had them in an outside pool. We couldn't very well leave them to fend for themselves in the hurricane, could we?

Off we go, headed inland, fish water splashing onto the carpet of the van at each turn. Truffles, always fastidious, refuses to put even one paw on the quickly soggy floor of the van. She rides perched on the tool box, which is in between the two captain's chairs in the front. Each time a turn causes a little more water to fly from the crest of a fishy wave and onto the floor, she gives a small, but clear "humph" and glares at us.

We really never were good enough for that dog.

By daybreak, we're about fifty miles inland. It's raining, and the wind is blowing, but nothing too impressive appears to be happening. We try to find a station on the van's radio to hear if the hurricane has hit land. We locate several, all in Spanish. All we can understand are the words *hurricano* and Cancun. This is not especially useful information.

Some of the people with whom we left camp decide to travel another hundred miles inland to the city of Merida. They figure they'll get a hotel room and hang out until the storm has passed. We decide to stay where we are. We play cards, walk around the tiny village, walk the dog, and pick the pig teeth out of the meat from the local taco stand where we're buying breakfast, lunch, and dinner.

By noon on the second day, the rain seems to have let up a little. We're tired of pig head tacos, the novelty of a dog covered in wrinkles has worn off for the local kids, and Jack decides to start cautiously back toward Paamul and see what we find.

I did warn you earlier about my dear husband's need to push the proverbial envelope, right?

Here's the thing.

The further we drive toward the coast, the harder the wind blows. Or so it seems to me.

But, when I mention this to Jack, he says, and this exact quote is burned indelibly into my memory banks, he says—and can you hear the tone of voice? Can you just envision that eyebrow cocked in frustration, the portrayal of exasperation at having to explain the way the world works to a woman?

He says, "Do you see that the wind is blowing counterclockwise?"

"No, not really," I say. "It just seems like it's blowing harder."

"Trust me, if it's blowing counterclockwise, then the hurricane has already passed."

"Well, see that's the thing, I'm pretty sure the clockwise/counterclockwise thing has to do with where we are in the world. And I don't guess I do actually trust you to interpret the conditions of a hurricane. *Since you've never seen one before!*"

That, more or less, is what I said.

Evidently, to a man, that actually means, "You have an extremely small penis, are an inadequate lover, and an all-around fuck up."

"I know what I'm doing," he retorts, and we keep heading for the coast.

A few tense minutes later, after he's dodged a fallen limb, after one of our windshield wiper blades, having been turned up to maximum speed, has flown off into the jungle, Jack says, "This is all just windfall from the hurricane. See? Proof the storm has passed."

Even Truffles can hear the uncertainty in his voice. The dog gives him a scornful look and one of her snorts.

It's just about now, as we're creeping along the obstacle course of fallen palm trees, that a policeman in a brown poncho runs up to our van, taps frantically on the driver's side window and begins yelling, "*Hurricano! Alto! Alto! Ven conmigo ahora!*" which, roughly translated means, "You fucked up and drove directly into the hurricane. Your wife is never going to let you forget it, and yes, you really do have a tiny little penis!"

We are shown where to pull our van off the side of the road and hurry toward a small cement schoolhouse. The officer clearly tells us to leave the dog in the car. I, just as clearly, make him understand that if the dog doesn't go, neither do I. With no time to argue, we bring the dog and step into the school house where we join a dozen Mayan families and a scattering of Mexican truck drivers and police officers. Standing room only. The toilet is a bucket in the corner of the room. There are a few pieces of soggy cardboard, scattered on the cement floor, which the children are using to make themselves little beds.

This is where we spend the next *thirty-eight hours*. The walls bend and bow, and the men line up and push from the inside to offset the winds on the outside. The children, at first frightened of Truffles and of us, settle in and use Jack as a shield at the height of the storm and the dog as a pillow. When the eye of the hurricane passes over, we all rush outside to pee and hurry back inside before the next wall of destruction hits. A person can't remain standing for thirty-eight hours, so long before the end is in sight, we're all curled together, lying in a foot or so of water and balancing the children along our bodies to keep them as dry as possible.

You get the idea.

When Jack says, "Trust me. I know what I'm doing,"—tone of voice and lifted eyebrow notwithstanding—I do get a teensy bit nervous. It's taken six years for his penis to reach its current size. We don't need to do anything to shrink the little guy again.

But I digress. Back in Arizona, I—the instigator of the plan to move to Panama—am getting nervous, while Jack is in full-speed-ahead mode. I can only pray we're not headed directly into the eye of yet another storm.

THREE
UNTRAINED JACKASSES AND THE LAUGHTER OF A SHIFTING BOULDER

TEN DAYS ON the market, and no one has even looked at the house. Then, the realtor calls to tell us a woman is coming from Scottsdale. She's seen the house on the internet and wants to buy it. We immediately envision hundred-dollar bills overflowing the pockets of some fool who wants to live in the high desert.

Two hours later, the house is sold.

The only catch is that the buyer wants to move in on November 1st. Just under a month away. Jack feels this is providence as—what a coincidence!—that's exactly the date of our tickets for the planned reconnaissance trip to Panama. I, on the other hand, am starting to feel the ominous rumblings of danger in the landscape.

I lobby for putting the dogs in a kennel for two weeks, making the planned trip with just the two of us and then, having set up a place to live temporarily, returning for the dogs. This is how that conversation went, to the best of my recollection.

"I'm *not* spending another two-thousand dollars on round-trip tickets to come back and get the dogs."

"But if we have the dogs with us, how are we going to explore the country?"

"I can take those dogs anyplace."

"You can take them in a taxi from the airport to a hotel?"

"Won't be a problem."

"You can get a hotel room with two giant dogs, in a country that has never heard of a service dog or the concept of taking an elephant-sized canine with you everywhere you go?"

"Won't be a problem."

"How are we going to fly them from Panama City to Bocas del Toro?"

"We'll buy them tickets on the plane if we have to. It won't be a problem. Why are you being so negative? Trust me."

Except—I don't. And Jack knows it, and his reaction to that is to get angry, and my reaction to his anger is to get more frightened and increasingly anxious. You can see where this is going, right? Can you almost hear the shifting of that rosy boulder?

———————

THE DOGS ARE accustomed to working one-on-one with Jack in any public situation, but they have never worked side-by-side. Jack is—predictably—sure this won't be a problem. However, former Marine, big tough warrior, whatever, like all intelligent men, he's a little afraid of his wife, so he humors me by bringing both dogs with us when we go out.

I handle Rocca. Jack takes Chesty.

For our trial outing, we go to the coffee shop where both dogs have been dozens of times. All the waitresses and regulars know them. We're in familiar territory. This little trip should be a breeze.

Both dogs act like untrained jackasses. Chesty shows off for Rocca by being hyper-alert to every little spoon-drop, cough, and loud voice. Rocca, trained to protect Jack, isn't happy about being next to me instead of within touching distance of the object of her devotion. She growls to intimidate Chesty who jumps up, stubby tail straight out and wagging, and barks loudly, *"Yeah, let's play!"* Rocca leaps up and growls and jumps in the middle of Chesty to show him who the real working dog around here is.

We leave the restaurant in disgrace.

Well actually, I'm the only one with her tail between her legs. The dogs have no regrets whatsoever, and Jack is impossible to embarrass. So, now we know. Working the dogs in tandem is a completely different deal than working them individually. Jack is pleased that we've found this out while we still have, let's see, twenty-four days before we lead them into the passenger section of a plane and fly to another country.

Did I not mention that these two dogs, because they are service dogs, will be flying in the passenger section of the plane with us? Take a minute and picture that.

How would you like to be the passenger next to us when we board the plane with these two massive dogs? United States law dictates that a disabled person can bring his dog on the airplane with him. Because both Chesty and Rocca are service dogs, and because I will be flying as a designated trainer/helper, both dogs will walk right up the ramp and board the plane at our sides. Jack is delighted with this. I am... less so.

The next twenty-four days go something like this:

I lie awake all night listening to Jack and the dogs snore and imagine all the ways this adventure can go terribly, irretrievably wrong.

The airline can, once we've arrived with the dogs at the check-in counter in Tucson, announce they've come to their senses and, of course, we can't board the plane with two monstrously large dogs.

The dogs can break away from us in the airport in Tucson, Houston, or Panama City and run amuck through the terminal, frightening old ladies in wheelchairs and spilling Starbucks coffee on men in business suits talking on cell phones with those stupid little earpiece things.

On arrival in Panama, customs can refuse to clear the dogs and take them away from us, where someone will steal them and enter them in dog fights. Chesty will be killed in the first fight as he tries to play with his opponent and misses completely the concept of the whole fight-to-the-death idea. Rocca will become the heavy-weight champion, and we'll hear rumors of her from time to time as we search ever more frantically for our furry baby girl.

We'll be unable to find a hotel in Panama City that will take the dogs, and we'll be spending our nights on the mean city streets of a foreign country, cuddled together in a big wadded mess of fear against a moldy cement wall.

Each dawn, I'm just about asleep when Chesty wakes me up.

"Did I hear a rabbit in the yard? I'm sure I heard a rabbit. Open the door quick so I can catch him. Hurry! Get up! Get up! Come on. The rabbit's getting away."

And another day begins.

Time to get rid of more earthly possessions. Salvation Army, friends, rummage sale customers, they all help us empty the house. We need to get rid of this crap and fast. We will be leaving with two suitcases each and two dogs. The biggest suitcase is already packed with dog food, dog harnesses and leashes, vitamins, glucosamine for their joints, and a couple of their favorite toys. My carry-on bag has liver treats for the plane to keep them entertained and to help with clearing their ears at take offs and landings. Every day is the same—keep moving toward the goal. Plenty of time at night to review all the things that can go wrong.

Here. *Right here*, is where an interesting thing begins to happen.

I edge beyond worry and begin to think, somewhere in the back of my overtaxed brain, that if I can anticipate all the things that might go wrong, I can prevent them from happening. This is when the jagged rocks directly above us begin to shift. You know the boulders I'm talking about, all those ordinary bits of life supporting that bone-crushing chunk of pink granite just waiting for gravity to trigger its descent.

If I hear the movement over all those wheels turning, turning, spinning faster and faster in my head, I interpret the rumbling of all that shifting rock as the grumbling of a nervous tummy.

I miss the warning completely and take a flying leap directly into that chasm named Obsessive Anxiety.

At this point, I mostly travel this rocky path in the dark. During the day, I do all the things I have to do to rid myself of all the stuff I thought I couldn't live without at varying times over the last six years when I accumulated it. By the way, standing at an airport in the pre-dawn hours with nothing to your name but two small suitcases, a day pack, your confident and smiling husband, and two large dogs, is an incredibly freeing experience. It's also absolutely terrifying.

FOUR

DON'T EVEN *THINK* ABOUT LOOKING AT EACH OTHER!

M Y BEST FRIEND, Mona, drives us to the Tucson airport on Halloween night. We're scheduled to fly out the next morning at what Jack calls "dawn-thirty." I hug Mona good-bye. She takes our picture. Two beat-to-crap suitcases, two scarred leather daypacks, two large, bright-eyed dogs, and two fools standing in front of the Days Inn, as ready as we're ever going to be for yet another adventure.

I can see Mona crying as she drives away. I'd love to join her in tears, but I need to concentrate on getting safely to our room with my suitcases and Rocca, for whom I'm responsible. Jack and I have worked daily with the dogs. Their behavior has improved, but mostly, they've trained us on how to handle them in tandem. Rocca has transferred some of her allegiance from Jack to me. This is good. It means she now looks to me for guidance instead of to him. Most of the time. We've learned to seat the dogs, whenever possible, back-to-back, not facing each other.

This is the move known as, "You look that way, and you look the other way. Don't even *think* about looking at each other!"

The problem with this solution, as all parents know, is that, sooner or later, you're going to hear the dreaded words, "He's looking at me!"

In our case, we would hear a low, rumbling growl that sounds more like the noise an enraged lion makes than anything that should come out of the throat of a domestic dog. This would be Rocca. Chesty would be peeking over his shoulder at her. Every time. His stubby tail jerking away, his eyes round and sparkling. The boy loves this game.

I have learned that once we hear the sound of the ground shaking with Rocca's warning, we have less than two seconds to prevent her from jumping up and into the middle of Chesty, giving him the exact feedback he seeks. You'll notice I said, "*I* have learned." Jack, on the other hand, learned that my nervousness and insistence on anticipating problems is causing the dogs to misbehave.

All right, so for now, we've gotten the dogs through the lobby and into the room at the Days Inn in Tucson without incident. Jack wants to take the dogs and go down the street to Burger King for dinner. I'm not leaving the room with both dogs unless I'm physically forced to do so. We compromise. We do it my way. He goes and gets burgers. I stay in the room with the dogs and attempt to convince myself that the shaking that overtakes me periodically is probably just excitement over the trip.

Cane Corso mastiffs have been bred as guard dogs for centuries in Italy. Our two have been raised on a five-acre patch of desert with the nearest road a mile away. People walking past our door in the night, bumping suitcases into walls or doing that loud whisper common to all drunks are the equivalent, to Chesty and Rocca, to a band of trained guerrillas sneaking in to execute us in our queen-size hotel bed. Rocca, like me, is a light sleeper. I spend most of the night sleeping with my hand on her head, ready to grab her snout and whisper, "No! Enough! Leave it! Stop! SSSSShhhhhhh! No!"

It feels like I never close my eyes, but truthfully, the snout grabbing thing probably didn't happen any more than a dozen times in this, our first of a long string of nights in hotel beds. Jack and Chesty, both able to sleep through a mortar attack, wake bright-eyed and bushy-tailed and ready for the day. Rocca and I shake ourselves into a blurry sleepwalk and away we go.

The dogs fall into formation in a heel beside us as soon as we buckle their working capes on them. Jack leads with Chesty, who's trying already to turn his head to look at Rocca, and Rocca lumbers along beside me, she and I grumbling at each step. Onto the shuttle bus we go and are delivered to the terminal just as the sun's light is beginning to reveal the silhouettes of the many-armed Saguaro cacti and desert palms around the airport. Inside, at the Continental check-in desk, the agents don't even blink at the dogs. Jack has spoken with the manager several times and also, as luck would have it, Randy Todd, who works in air traffic control and is the breeder from whom we bought Chesty, is at the check-in counter.

Besides this lucky occurrence, many people at the Tucson airport are familiar with both Chesty and Rocca as we've brought them here often as part of their training over the years. Several of the security guards come over to say good-bye. Chesty takes all this attention with wiggling dignity until the flight attendant arrive. Then he throws himself on the floor, rolls over on his back, and presents his best side for rubbing. Rocca and I stand back and watch this foolish display of unprofessional behavior while Jack's voice booms around the terminal announcing to everyone that we're moving to Panama. Yes, the country, not the city in Florida.

This is as good a time as any to tell you that while Jack loves to be the center of attention, I am happiest when I can come and go and no one even notices I've been there. Taking the dogs with us everywhere puts us firmly in Jack's glory and miles outside my comfort zone. Having taken not one, but *two* giant dogs with us every single time we've left the house, on absolutely every errand and excursion for the last month in order to accustom them to working together has left me a tad grumpy.

All right, let me modify that self-assessment—I'm already a flaming bitch, and we haven't even gotten on the plane yet.

By the time we line up at the boarding gate, it's full daylight, and I'm saying a silent goodbye to the clear blue desert sky under which I've lived for the last six years. Jack is explaining to the passenger in line in front of us that he's going to breed these dogs in Panama and sell them to rich Latin Americans who will pay any price to get them. Chesty is prancing along in full, handsome, working-dog mode. Rocca is looking up at me and asking with her eyes, "Last chance. Are you absolutely *sure* this is a good idea?"

Okay. I'm probably projecting that attitude onto her, but she really does look a little nervous.

Knowing that she'll take her cue from me, I pat her huge head and tell her, "Sure, no problem. We can easily leap clear of this little crevasse. Not to worry."

The dog still seems like she's wondering if she's going to be chewing off her leg before this whole adventure has ended, but she lumbers along obediently beside me.

When we find our bulkhead seats on the plane and I see the tiny space into which the dogs are expected to fit, I turn to Jack and declare in my firmest voice, "This isn't going to work."

Unfortunately, Jack's still telling his new friend about the history of the Cane Corso breed and how they were trained by Italian ranchers to grab the bull by the nose and hold the huge animal while the farmer cut the throat at butchering time. My husband pays no attention whatsoever to his panicked wife. Rocca and I are pushed forward into our assigned seats. I am against the window. Jack has the aisle seat. I instruct Rocca to lie at my feet, wedged in between the seat and the bulk head, with her head facing toward the outside of the plane. My feet rest on Rocca's back. Chesty lies with his head sticking out into the aisle. The dogs are butt-to-butt. Okay. This is uncomfortable, but it might work. If the flight from Tucson to Houston isn't any longer than ten minutes.

"Jack," I say in a quiet voice, trying to keep the panic smashed down where it will only eat a hole in my stomach lining instead of leaping out my throat and spilling all over the inside of the airplane. "I don't think this is going to work."

"What? See, nothing to worry about. The dogs fit just fine in this space," he says with his usual enthusiasm for impossibly difficult situations.

Maybe it's just me. But flying with both of these dogs in the passenger section at our feet—this is a sane idea?

Now the situation moves beyond difficult, and I am absolutely, positively sure we've crossed that demarcation line into full-fledged-screaming-crazy-land-wacky-this-can't-be-doneville. The head flight attendant tells Jack that Chesty's head cannot extend out into the aisle. People might trip over him. Which means that one of the dogs is going to have to lie *on top of the other dog.*

No way Rocca is going to allow Chesty to lie on top of her, so we maneuver ourselves out of our seats. This proves the most difficult for Rocca as she is stuck and has to grunt and groan and look balefully up at me until she manages to wiggle her way out of this predicament into which we have placed her. Once in the aisle, we think our way through this arrangement like those big-footed clowns at the circus trying to fit into the Volkswagen before the start of the greatest show on earth.

Chesty has to be able to see out the aisle. He's had far too much training in watching Jack's back to handle anything else. Rocca has to be the dog on top. The dogs have to be placed so that Chesty can't look at Rocca and stir her up into a froth of irritation. All right, let's try this.

I squeeze into the tiny space between the seats and the bulkhead wall with Rocca, and she sits while Chesty and Jack get into position with Chesty's butt extending to the front of my seat. Then Rocca lies down with her butt on top of Chesty's haunches. Yeah. This is just perfect. I can't see why this isn't going to work for the four-hour flight to Houston. Both dogs look as though they are going to begin a serious search for new owners the moment we get off the plane. My feet are now perched on Rocca's back, which is on top of Chesty's back.

Then things get interesting. There is a passenger in the aisle who claims to have a ticket for the middle seat, the seat between Jack and me. An older woman who's on her way to visit her grandchildren for the week. There are no other seats available. Jack gets up, Chesty goes with him, Rocca sits up. The poor woman seats herself in the middle seat. Rocca lies down. On the woman's feet. I have Rocca get up, freeing the woman. The old lady puts her feet up on the seat.

"See how this is going to work out?" Jack says brightly. "Who'd have thought we'd be so lucky as to end up next to a woman agile enough at her age to sit with her feet perched up on the seat like that?"

Jack sits and then backs Chesty into his space. Rocca lies down, wedging herself yet again into her allotted space on top of Chesty. Chesty looks goofily around, his rump pinned, his tongue hanging from the side of his mouth.

"Are we having fun Dad? Is this the adventure you've been telling me about? Huh? Is it? Huh?"

I apologize to the woman, who tells us that this will be a wonderful story to tell her grandchildren. Sure, as soon as the feeling comes back into her legs and she can actually exit the plane. Jack tells her the holding-the-bull-by-the-nose story, and I don't even interrupt to ask why in hell the farmer would be butchering a bull. Wouldn't it be a steer he'd be killing? Somehow this detail just doesn't seem like a relevant point at the moment.

Remember those treats we brought so the dogs would be chewing and swallowing at takeoff and landing? These turn out to be a really bad idea. First of all, getting anything out of my daypack, which is on my lap, means moving around at least a little and there really is no room to move. No room at all.

But more importantly Rocca has decided, in true female fashion, that all of her difficulties are the fault of this stupid male dog on whose butt she's being forced to lie. Not only does she not believe he is worthy of a treat, she doesn't think he should be allowed to live. The instant I break the seal and she smells the liver, she starts one of those low elephant rumbles of which I am all too familiar. I correct her, stuff the liver treats back in the backpack and beg the flight attendant to put the pack in the overhead compartment instead of on my lap where the smells are going to waft down and cause a scene I am desperately praying to avoid.

Rocca settles down and, in this fashion, several lifetimes later, we make it to Houston. The old lady's grandchildren are there to greet her at the gate, and she introduces us and the dogs to everyone. How else would they possibly believe her story? After meeting her family, we make our way to the gate for our Continental flight to Panama City. We check in and again, no official blinks at the two dogs with whom we'll be boarding. Evidently, as long as something, anything, is on the computer screen, it's no problem. Now, sitting in those plastic chairs that are all attached together and to the floor, we lose our concentration for a moment, and Chesty turns around and *looks at Rocca*.

Rocca, already madder than the proverbial wet hen, leaps up and jumps into the middle of this stinkin' male dog who is the cause of all her freakin' problems. Every single damn one.

Chesty wiggles his tail and does his "Aren't I the cutest thing you've ever seen" routine, and I correct Rocca and move her away from Chesty. The whole episode takes no more than three seconds. It clears all the seats around us for a good thirty feet.

Jack and I act as though this is no big deal. Nothing to worry about. We move the dogs and go right on with our conversation about who should go and get us a Starbucks coffee. Amazingly it works, and the flight attendant lets us board the plane with both dogs where—the good news is—there's no one in the middle seat between us. And the bad news is—Rocca has now decided that that freakin' boy dog had better not even *think* of looking at her.

FIVE
ROCCA AND I GROW GRUMPY
OKAY—GRUMPIER

AS WE WALK the covered ramp to enter the second plane of the day, the flight that will take us out of the country and to our new home in Panama, I am at that stage of exhaustion and anxiety known as "walking comatose."

Again, I take the window seat with Rocca. I put her in a sit and physically hold her head against my chest so she can't turn and look at Chesty as he, happy as the proverbial clam, backs into his spot and eases himself down. Convincing Rocca to lie with her rump resting cockeyed up on top of Chesty is a challenge. She's done this before and didn't enjoy the procedure in the least. Putting my dog in position without her or the ever-playful Chesty turning their heads to make eye contact leaves me shaking and twitching, but we eventually get both dogs adjusted with a couple of airplane blankets under Rocca's head to even out her position a little. Jack and I each throw one leg over the necks of our dogs so as to prevent them turning and, God forbid, looking at each other.

Rocca is already rumbling in the knowledge that Chesty is, sure enough, trying his hardest to twist around to see what kind of reaction he can get out of her. I bend over with her head held tightly against my chest and whisper to her what we'll do to both males once we're on the ground and safe somewhere. She and I stay that way, making our plans, until the plane is in the air. I don't tell my furry girl that I have no idea when we'll be anywhere that resembles safety.

Once the plane is in the air, Jack leans over to me and says, "We're home free now. What are they gonna do? Throw us off the plane?"

He then strikes up a conversation with three men in Hawaiian shirts across the aisle who are flying down to Panama for their yearly month-long fishing trip. These guys seem to know more about the gentlemen's clubs in the city than they do about sailfish or dorado, but perhaps they've only heard rumors about such things. Jack tells them about his plans to raise guard dogs in Panama. I on the other hand spend most of the flight worrying about getting through customs once we land, and don't completely believe the pilot will not turn the plane around in a swooping U and carry Jack and me and the dogs back to the land of Federal Marshalls until the flight attendant tells us we're over halfway through our flight. Then I concentrate all my anxiety on the ordeal of getting the dogs through customs and out of the airport.

The requirements for entering the Republic of Panama with an animal are complicated. You need an international health certificate. We were lucky and our veterinarian on Fort Huachuca was familiar with these documents and actually had them on hand along with the official stamp that is required. Once in our possession, this piece of paper had to be Overnight FedExed to the Panamanian consulate in Houston for their official stamp and signature. This all had to be done so that the dates of the stamps were no more than ten days from the time of our arrival in the country. We did all that. Those papers are in my daypack.

On arrival, we will need to have the government veterinarian approve this paperwork, examine the dogs, and sign off before we'll be allowed to leave the airport with Chesty and Rocca. Our flight arrives in Panama at 7:45 p.m. The vet works eight to five. However, he has been contacted by our realtor and asked to stay until after he checks us through customs because we refuse to leave our dogs overnight in the airport. The vet has reportedly agreed to stay and examine the dogs for the low, low cost of fifty dollars. Which we gladly agreed to pay.

There is supposed to be someone meeting us when we arrive. Here's how that happened. We sold our house through our local RE/MAX company.

The realtor in Arizona asked if we wanted a referral to a RE/MAX agent in the area where we were relocating.

I jokingly said, "Sure, fix that up for us. We're moving to the Republic of Panama."

Turns out there is a RE/MAX office in Panama and our agent hooked us up with a nice, unsuspecting young man named Arie. This poor guy has been our contact person ever since. He's the one who talked to the veterinarian at the airport, and he's the one who begged a friend at a hotel to rent a room to us and our two giant service dogs.

At least, we hope he's done all this. We've only spoken with him on the phone, and I can already tell we're making him half-crazy with our weird requests and questions. He's been gallant and accommodating, but for all I know, we'll never see him once we land and nothing has actually been pre-arranged at the airport or the hotel.

Well, you can see that I entertain myself with lovely, rosy thoughts on the three-and-a-half hour flight from Houston to Panama City. I do supplement these images of impending disaster with holding Rocca's head when Chesty's wagging tail sets off her rumblings. I also break the monotony by digging my fingers into Jack's arm, making little squeaking moans, and saying things like:

"What if the vet's not there?"

"Do you know the name of the hotel where we're supposed to be staying?"

"Watch your dog! He's looking at mine!"

"If the vet's not there, I'm not leaving my dogs!"

"I have to pee, but there's no way I can leave Rocca and make my way to the bathroom."

"I hope Arie is there to meet us."

"Chesty's looking at Rocca!"

"If Arie's not there, how are we going to even get to the hotel?"

"Where is this hotel in relation to the airport?"

"I really have to pee."

Jack's response to all of this is predictable.

"Don't worry. Everything will be fine. There won't be any problems that we can't handle. Did you hear what the guy said about the fifty-dollar lunch special at the gentleman's club?"

I have gone now beyond comatose and into the altered state of consciousness where the mantra, "One breath at a time. One breath at a time," has brought me to a place where peace and calm are attempting to beat the crap out of the crazed lunatic who seems to be lodged somewhere at about the level of my gut.

Flying into the city at night, skyscrapers light a black curve of bay, and the Bridge of the Americas over the canal is strung with colored jewels like something from a fairyland. The low clouds race in the wind and create the illusion that the plane is standing still and the city itself is moving, flowing along in another world down below us. I relax a little. Maybe our new home is going to be okay. Maybe Jack's right and everything really will be fine. Maybe pigs really can sprout wings and fly.

Once on the ground, while everyone else is racing for the customs line I walk Rocca, both of us stiff-legged, to the nearest bathroom. By the time we leave the facilities, I feel much better, but Rocca has still not been outside to pee since we left Tucson this morning before dawn. Getting both dogs outside has become a priority.

Unfortunately, we need to clear customs before we can leave the building. This is expedited for us when the veterinarian comes to greet us as we wait in line. We are easy to spot. We're the people with the crowd of giggling porters surrounding us, wanting to see the two big dogs that we've actually brought in the passenger section of the plane with us. The vet and his assistant introduce themselves and take us to the front of the customs line. This seems unfair to those other folks waiting, but I let it pass.

We are now in possession of two big, active dogs who have had no exercise and no opportunity to pee for fourteen hours. Chesty is absolutely goofy with pent up energy. He bounces along beside Jack, looking at the people, his tail in constant circular motion. Rocca walks stiff-legged, plotting her revenge on Chesty, whom she is intent on blaming for all the difficulties of her long hard day. Gee, I wonder where she gets *that* attitude from?

Jack and I are careful to keep our own bodies between the two dogs as neither of us trust Rocca not to tear into Chesty, or Chesty not to provoke her just to get some action going. At this point, the vet tells Jack to leave the dogs with me. Jack must go with three officials to fill out paperwork and pay the money needed to get us the hell out of the airport.

Here's the thing. I can control one of these dogs, but not both of them if they decide to act up—and they've already decided to act up. Rocca is doing a near-constant low rumble and Chesty's eyes are round and sparkling and he's itching for a chance to play.

Putting Rocca in a sit, I tie Chesty to a steel rail bolted into the marble floor of the terminal. I move slightly away from Chesty and, making sure I'm in between the two dogs, tell the boy to sit. He looks at me like he's never heard that particular command before. Could I maybe say it again, or better yet, bring that rumbly girl dog over here a little closer while I make him do what I've told him to do? I ignore him in the hope that he'll settle down, pray Jack won't be gone long.

A porter is escorting our luggage through customs. The inspectors open the largest bag and discover the dog food, dog toys, and other assorted doggie paraphernalia. This causes the officials to call over all the other inspectors. The checkout line comes to a stand-still while five men in uniform peer down into our luggage. Are they going to tell me that we can't bring dog food into the country? No. They've just never actually seen anyone stupid enough to bring a giant bag of dog food in a suitcase and figure it has to be seen to be believed.

Eventually the other passengers have left the terminal, and the porters entertain themselves by teasing the dogs. These playful gentlemen challenge each other to see who's brave enough to get close to Chesty who is wagging that abbreviated tail in tight circles and begging for an opportunity to play. This little game of chicken ends abruptly when one of the porters gets too close, Chesty lunges and the steel rail to which I've tied him comes unbolted from the tile floor. Before it can come completely loose, bringing to fruition my nightmare of my dog running amuck in the airport terminal, knocking people over and having a slobbery, good-old-time while the police come to haul us all away, I manage to grab the leash. I have visions of having to pay for the broken rail, but the audience's reaction seems to be that this is a hilarious happening and why don't I tie him up again so the dogs can return to their fun game?

Now I have both dogs on leashes, one in each hand. Rocca—thank you Jesus—has decided that Chesty is too stupid for the likes of her to even bother to interact with, and she is behaving wonderfully. Chesty, on the other hand, is bursting with excitement and energy. Another plane has arrived, bringing a whole new group of passengers as well as two crated dogs. The crates are placed directly in front of me and my two dogs.

You know that old saying about how two brothers fight, but when a cousin shows up, it's the two brothers against the cousin. And when a neighbor shows up, it's the two brothers and the cousin against the neighbor. Well, it works that way with dogs, too.

The dogs in the crates are yellow labs. No sweeter, more clueless dog exists. They bark a greeting to Chesty and Rocca.

"Hey! How come you're not in a little doggie jail like us?"

Chesty, all but vibrating with joy, answers, *"Wanna play? Do ya? Do ya? Huh? Huh?"*

Rocca, giant head up, stiff with annoyance chimes in with, *"Don't you come near me. I'll tear you a new one if you so much as look at me."*

The yellow labs are now frantic to interact and they have a chorus of, *"Let us out! Let us out! Let us out!"* going nonstop.

Chesty lunges toward the crates while I use an old dog-trainer trick of which I'm not proud but that is effective in situations just like this. I lift him straight up off the ground by his collar, causing him to have to choose between lunging or breathing. He chooses breathing. But, remember, he was named after a Marine, and he forgets the lesson basically one breath after I set him down. So we repeat the experience a dozen or so times as I back him and Rocca slowly away from the yellow labs.

By the time Jack returns with the paperwork stamped, signed, and approved, I have both dogs across the terminal. Chesty is doing one of his loud whines, and Rocca is rumbling like a volcano about to spew molten lava on everything in its path. All the passengers from the last flight of the night have been processed through and are gone. My arms and shoulders feel as though I've climbed Mount Everest. Plus, I have to pee again.

Once outside the terminal, we discover that all the taxis have left for the day. The Tocumen International Airport is about ten miles outside the city of Panama. However, lo and behold, here comes Arie—our realtor and best friend in the whole wide world. He has been waiting for us for the two hours it took us to clear customs. We love him. We would like to adopt him. He will give us a ride in his shiny, black SUV to the Las Vegas Suites, which is where he's finagled a room for us and the dogs.

First things first, however. I take Rocca to the nearest palm tree where she squats and pees for a full five minutes. Jack, who is talking with Arie, doesn't notice what Chesty is doing until the stream of urine is already flowing in a golden river from the back tire of the spotlessly clean vehicle in which we are hoping to catch a ride to the hotel.

"Ha, ha, ha," says Jack. "He really had to go!"

Arie, now silent, evidently isn't a dog person.

The luggage loaded, we next need to get the dogs inside the SUV. Jack gets in the front passenger seat and, with no invitation at all, Chesty leaps into the car and sits in Jack's lap. This is not where our new best friend anticipated this 110-pound dog would be riding.

"Ha, ha, ha," says Jack. "That's my boy."

I now make a mistake.

I tell Rocca to get in the back seat before I am in the car. She jumps in. Chesty turns from his place on Jack's lap and *looks at her*. Arie, already in the driver's seat, is starting the car while talking into his cell phone. Rocca comes across the front passenger seat and into Chesty's face with a growl that sets off the alarm on the car parked in front of us. Chesty—finally rewarded for all his struggles to get a rise out of her—barks in excitement and jumps so that he's standing on Jack's chest with his head hanging over the seat. Arie levitates out of the car and is halfway across the parking lot and still moving in the second and a half it takes me to correct and control Rocca and for Chesty to reseat himself, his tongue hanging from his mouth, his eyes glittering with good fun.

"Ha, ha, ha," Jack calls to the still-running Arie. "That scared you a little, huh?"

Eventually, we coax Arie back in the car with the promise that the dogs will behave perfectly for the rest of the ride to the city. I hold Rocca's head against my chest and talk to her all the way while Jack talks to a strangely quiet Arie, and Chesty looks vigorously to the left at the bay and to the right at the skyscrapers, thus throwing a good bit of slobber onto the windows and leather seats of the Prada.

When we arrive at the Las Vegas Suites, it turns out to be a seven-story high-rise. The handicapped room on the top floor has been reserved for us. The night manager panics when he sees the dogs, but Arie calls his friend the day manager, on his cell phone and she instructs the night supervisor to rent us a room. We sign the register under the large sign which proclaims, in Spanish, "Absolutely no dogs allowed in the hotel."

Arie hands me a RE/MAX card and explains he will be leaving town unexpectedly, but that a new guy, Leo, will be happy to help us find a place to live or anything else we might need. He starts to walk away and then returns to let me know that his cell phone number will not be working for the next few months as he will be out of the service area. So, if we have any questions, just call Leo. Not him.

The elevator in this high-rise is glass. Chesty high-steps inside and whines at the people eating in the courtyard restaurant below. He is delighted with this new adventure. Rocca flattens herself like a cat and squeezes her eyes shut. The porter dumps our baggage in the room, and we ride the elevator back down to walk some of the energy out of the dogs. Rocca and I are quiet on our little two-mile jaunt. Jack and Chesty are pumped with adrenaline. Chesty finds four cats and two hookers with whom to interact, and he's a happy pup by the time we get back to our room. The cats, by the way, appear to hate him, while the prostitutes love him.

As I fall asleep with my hand on Rocca's wide snout to prevent her from barking at the folks walking by the room, the last thing I hear is Jack, who rolls over and throws his arm over me and says, "See, that wasn't so bad, was it?"

SIX
THE END OF A STRAIGHT LINE
OR (MY FAVORITE) WHEN THE BALLS ARE BIGGER THAN THE BRAIN

T HE LAS VEGAS Suites is located at the cusp of the Financial District and the El Cangrejo section of the city. Both areas are safe, day or night, tree-lined and inundated with visual surprises, glorious dress shops and mansions just visible through curlicued wrought iron gates. Our hotel is a block from the busy, shop-lined Via España. El Reyes Supermarket is a fifteen-minute, sweat-soaked walk away. A dozen wonderful restaurants are within walking distance.

But I don't know any of this when I open my eyes my first morning in the country. What I do know is that the casino across the street, the Veneto, sets off what sounds like incoming mortar rounds whenever a customer wins over two dollars. Day and night. I've also already discovered the most important piece of equipment on any vehicle inching along in the Panama City traffic is its horn, which needs to be leaned on continually. My third piece of information about my new environment is that our little suite at the Las Vegas is clean and adequate and last decorated about the time I was born.

Jack takes the dogs out, one at a time, for a quick pee and then brings me coffee from downstairs. I'm still curled in bed with the covers over my head when I hear him come in singing, "Young girl, get outta my mind, your love for me is way overpriced."

"Morning, Love, here's your coffee in bed."

I'm glad he's happy, but that big grin on his face is truly irritating.

My doting husband claims that we have a deal, an agreement, that he will bring me two cups of coffee each morning of our married lives, and I will do everything else. This is not exactly how I remember the agreement, but then, I should have gotten it in writing. At the moment, I just want my coffee.

"Thanks," I croak as I sit up and push the pillows behind me as a backrest. "Where'd you get it?"

"Free coffee every morning. All we want. Downstairs in the restaurant in the courtyard."

Anything free makes Jack happy. It doesn't have to be usable or eatable or drinkable, just free.

"After you have your coffee, we'll take the dogs for a walk and explore the area a little. I met a guy downstairs who's here looking for property in Boquete. It's up in the mountains toward Costa Rica. There's another couple here from Wisconsin looking for beach property on the Pacific side of the country."

He says a bunch of other stuff, too, but all I really hear is, "I'm excited about being here. It's completely reasonable to be relocating to Panama because I've already met other seemingly normal people who are here to do the same thing as us. I have no clue that the thought of walking outside again with the dogs is making my wife's hand shake sufficiently enough to spill coffee on the bedspread. Nor am I aware that the twitch over her eye has come back."

Once I have my second cup of coffee, I shower, dress, and force myself to venture outside. And immediately remember something about Latin America. They don't do straight lines or hard and fast rules. There are no sharp-edged curbs or right-of-ways when crossing the street. Just weave through traffic and don't get hit. We're in a handicapped room which is fitted perfectly for someone in a wheelchair. But once outside the lobby of the hotel, there's no way a person in a wheelchair could get around. Sidewalks have gaping holes into which Rocca stares, watching the black water flowing sluggishly along on its way to, presumably, the bay.

When I stop to look in a shop window at custom-made dresses, beautiful and elegant enough to be worn to the Oscars, black water drips on my head from the balcony above. Kuna Indians, the women in beaded leg wraps with silver rings in their noses, have quilts and paintings displayed on the sidewalks. Beside them, Caribbean blacks wearing high, puffy red and green crocheted reggae hats are selling beaded bracelets and clay pipes. Chinese are everywhere, chattering away to each other in their own complex language.

All this in the thick, soupy heat of smog and concrete. Horns blare continually, every five minutes or so someone wins at one of the casinos, and they set off noise makers from hell. The dogs are doing great. They trot right beside us as we weave our way through the city. This is made easier by the fact that, when people see us coming, they clear the area. Evidently, big dogs here in Panama are guard dogs. Vicious attack guard dogs. Walking them on a crowded city sidewalk causes mothers to grab their children and flee. Everyone else steps off the sidewalk and into the street to give us plenty of room.

Rocca is taking this in stride. She looks up at me more than usual, but that may be because she's trying to locate the cause of the shaking that's transmitting down her leash. Chesty is puzzled. He's never been out in public without people fussing over him, petting him, telling him what a handsome boy he is. Every time he sees a pretty woman approaching, he wags that tail and bounces along in anticipation, only to have the young lady vacate the sidewalk and risk being run over to get away from him.

The other thing I notice on this first walk in the city is that the trees are beautiful here. They make a canopy of leafy green over nearly every street. Everything is dirtier than it would be in an American city. Or, at least, in any part of an American city where I'd feel safe walking. Curbs are crumbled, manhole covers are missing, construction has created large gaps in sidewalks and streets, these traps left to ensnare whoever is careless enough to fall in. Black mold defaces the concrete of a high-rise apartment building where many of the balconies are softened with green plants and talking parrots in fancy iron cages.

We walk for an hour and then stop at a restaurant, Manolos, just down from the hotel. They have an air-conditioned dining room, but we sit outside on the spacious patio. The dogs back themselves under the table. Chesty peeks out. Even on vacation, he's working. Rocca seems to have decided that if

Chesty's on duty, she's taking a nap. By the time the waitresses decide among themselves who has to wait on us, Rocca's snoring loudly. The oldest waitress in the place brings our menus. I suppose she's already lived more of her life than the others, so the risk of death is less worrisome. Jack tries to assure her that the dogs are well-behaved and will be no problem.

I don't know if she believes him any more than I do.

My husband decides on the "Panama Breakfast Special," and I have a cup of cappuccino. I'm afraid to put anything in my stomach right at the moment, what with the little gremlin crawling around in there grumbling, "Stupid, stupid, stupid. Why did you think moving here would be a good idea? Stupid, stupid, stupid."

"So, what do you think so far?" Jack asks. His eyes sparkle, and he looks around with pretty much the same attitude as Chesty.

"It's very cosmopolitan," I say. "I've never been to a place where people from so many different countries seem to be living side by side. Well, except New York City. New York was filled with lots of different nationalities, I guess."

"Yeah," Jack agrees with me. "Panama City is called 'The New York City of Central America.'"

"By who?" I ask in what I'm afraid is a very snotty voice. Then, in case he missed my point, I follow that up with, "By people who've never been to New York City, maybe."

We decide then that we've visited with each other enough for the moment and focus on the traffic creeping by and the beautifully dressed people stepping around obstacles until the waitress brings our order.

The cappuccino looks wonderful. Thick foam in a fat, bright yellow cup. Jack's breakfast seems to be tough meat in tomato-based sauce with something that looks like hoecakes from his southern childhood. Before we can sample any of this, a woman walks by accompanied by a toy poodle with a death wish. The poodle peeks in through the rail of the restaurant and spots Chesty.

"Yo! Big foreign fool! You are funny-looking and what's that stupid cape your people have stuck on your black ass?" Or something similar. The French dog yaps and yips as his owner tugs him on past us.

Chesty—wonderfully trained service dog though he may be—is, you will remember, named for a Marine. He leaps up, bangs his head on the underside of the table, and spills my cappuccino. His tail wags in tight circles, his ears straight up, his eyes round and glittering.

"Wait!" barks Chesty. *"Come back! I know a game we can play called 'Pack the little poofy French moron in my mouth!' It's fun. Come on back and play."*

The poodle, whose balls are far bigger than his brain, tears the leash from his mistress's hand and streaks back to the rail which he attempts to scale with his little short pom pom-adorned legs.

Chesty encourages him with, *"Come on, come on, come on! Bring your fluffy, white ass up here where I can reach you!"*

The sight of the waitresses huddled together inside the restaurant and the people at the outside tables staring open-mouthed at all this is being permanently stamped onto my memory.

Rocca, awakened from her nap by all this hoopla, lifts her entire 148-pound body in one stiff-legged surge.

"Enough!" she growls.

Dishes rattle, waitresses squeal, and the poodle, who sees Rocca for the first time, flips himself over backwards and throws himself into the arms of his owner.

"Ha, ha, ha," says Jack. *"Solamente jugando."* Which may or may not mean, "Only playing."

Rocca and I exchange a look. Chesty lies back down.

Jack finishes his breakfast. "Hey! These fried corn cake things are good. You want a taste?"

The shaking has subsided on the right side of my body enough that I can almost get my cup to my mouth without spilling it, so I just jerk my head from side to side in answer.

BACK IN THE room, the dogs collapse and try to recover from the heat, I go back to bed, and Jack sets off to see what he can do to get us to our next stop—Bocas del Toro. The plan is to head to the islands as soon as we can get a flight. Once there, we'll stay in a hotel until we find a place to buy.

Curled up under the covers, the air-conditioner doing its best to block out the noise of horns and the casino, I try to think my way through this anxiety that is eating me up. This is not the first time Jack and I have traveled. We've been to Asia—twice. We spent three months each time, traveling around on local buses with nothing but a daypack each. I loved those trips. The first trip, we concentrated on Thailand and Malaysia, and the second trip, we did Nepal, Vietnam, and the parts of Thailand we missed on the first trip. Yes, I got overwhelmed from time to time, and we spent a day or two just laying around a funky little hotel recovering from the culture shock. But I've never had this kind of runaway anxiety before. Never.

What's different is that, this time, we have the dogs. Big dogs who, it feels to me, we've put in danger by bringing. Dogs that don't have any business in a high-rise hotel or on streets as frantically busy as these. Dogs that are now in a country where they are not protected by the disability laws we have in the States and where people are not required to allow them into restaurants or taxis or planes or hotels. Dogs that I love and for whom I am responsible. Dogs that, if they are harmed I will never, ever, ever forgive myself.

Okay. This thinking-through-the-anxiety idea doesn't seem to be working. Good decision or bad, we're here now, and I need to deal with the reality of our situation. Nothing terrible has really happened. We have a hotel room. The restaurant didn't ask us to leave and never return. So far, Jack's right. We're managing. Things are working out.

As long as one of the dogs doesn't escape when the maids come in to clean or jerk the leash out of Jack's hand because he insists on laying it across his lap when he's eating instead of wrapping it sixteen times around a hand like I do, we'll be okay. If we can get the dogs to Bocas del Toro, if we can find a place to stay and then a place to buy once we get there, we'll be all right. If we can find a place to buy that has a secure fence, where the dogs can't get out and no one can steal them, then we'll be safe.

I double-check the hotel room door to be sure it's locked. The dogs and I are safe at the moment. Except isn't that Jack I hear coming down the hall singing, "Raindrops keep falling on my head, but doesn't mean I won't still be screwing you, nothing can stop that, no...?"

SEVEN
WE NEED A BETTER MAP

WE SEEM TO have made a slight miscalculation.

Again.

November is Panama's Independence month. In theory, not the entire month, but in practice—the whole freakin' month is a holiday.

November 1st is National Anthem Day.

November 2nd is All Souls Day—which to me has nothing obviously patriotic about it but is nonetheless included in the holiday.

November 3rd is Independence from Colombia Day.

November 10th is First Cry of Independence from Spain Day, also called "Los Santos Uprising Day."

November 28th is Independence from Spain Day.

All the days in between are either prepare for the holiday or recover from the party days.

Yet another thing about the country we didn't know is that on any and all holidays people flee the city in great flocks and go to the beaches. Bocas del Toro is a favorite spot. You have to get plane tickets six months in advance for the month of November. A little fact that any Panamanian knows, and these two clueless *gringos* never even considered.

Now what?

"It's not a problem," says Jack. "Since we can't get a flight, we'll just take a taxi. Panama isn't all that big. How far can it be to the other side of the country?"

We spread our map out on the table. It looks like there are roads going up into the mountains from the Pacific coast Pan-American Highway, but then this map doesn't show any roads connecting to any other roads. Each red line indicating a highway or trail or road ends in the mountains, sometimes only a few miles from another road that goes from the highway to some other little mountain town.

"We need a better map," Jack says.

"Look at this whole Caribbean coast," I say. "It's as if there are no roads there at all. How funny. People can't take boats along the coast and then walk for a hundred miles to the nearest road! That's ridiculous."

"Ha, ha, ha," both white-skinned idiots say.

Jack goes back out in search of a real map. One that shows the small connecting roads that will get us to Bocas del Toro. He takes Chesty with him and leaves Rocca with me.

There's something else I need to tell you about these dogs. When you take the leashes off them, they become deaf. Totally deaf. They can be standing, let's see, how long is my arm? Let's say grabbing distance is three feet. So, the dog can be three feet and a half inch away, and Jack or I can be shouting pretty much at the top of our lungs, and neither dog can hear us. Evidently, not one screeching tone pierces its way through their ears and into their brains. Without the leashes, they are wild and crazy deaf dogs.

This, for me, changes everything. It means I am thinking constantly about where my dogs are, how many doors are between them and freedom, who might open that door and unknowingly release them out into the world of havoc, death, law suits, and foreign jails where you have to catch and cook cockroaches over a fire kindled from the tennis shoes that you steal from the dead body of your fellow prisoner who the guards have beaten to death.

Did I mention that I crossed over the line into obsessive anxiety miles and miles ago? Is that becoming more and more clear to you?

So Jack takes Chesty, the leash held loosely in his non-obsessive hand, and goes in search of a better map. One that conforms to our expectations of the country. Rocca isn't happy about being left behind. Or else she has to go to the bathroom. Chesty has eaten almost nothing since we left Arizona.

Rocca, on the other hand, is a swell eater. In fact, she seems to eat when she's hungry, when she's bored, when she's upset, when she's happy, or sad. Again, I have no idea where she gets this behavior. But since she's increasingly insistent about going out, I may as well walk her to the corner store and see if I can find some chocolate. And maybe a bag of potato chips.

Rocca swings her head along from side to side as we head for the elevator. She's gotten her routine down now for riding in the glass cage. As I insert the room key card and push the button, she sprawls out with her belly touching the floor, holds her breath, and squeezes her eyes tight. At least this trip in the glass jail she doesn't have Chesty's enthusiasm for the experience to contend with. When the elevator doors slide open, I hear Jack's voice. Rocca's already heard him, and she lifts her head, her ears cocked forward in search mode.

My husband is standing in the lobby, talking with what appears to be the entire female staff of the hotel. Three young women have cameras. They're posing for pictures with Chesty. None of the chicas are brave enough to take his leash. When Rocca and I step off the elevator, Jack is in between two young ladies, his arm high on the waist of each one—though not being the jealous type, I hardly notice this detail. I do note that, when he looks up and sees me, he does one of those miniscule startle-hops known to all husbands as, "Who-ya-gonna-believe? Me-or-your-eyes?"

"Hey! Here's my lovely wife! And Rocca. Would any of you lovely young ladies like your picture taken with Rocca?"

The young ladies in question decline this invitation and scurry back to work.

"Did you find a better map?"

"A what? Oh. No. Not yet."

He gives me a sheepish grin and a hug.

"I'm glad you came down," he lies blatantly. "Let's walk the dogs and explore a little."

Which we do. Traffic is lighter today. It appears that everyone who can get there is already at their beach house. Crossing the streets, weaving between traffic, we narrowly miss death only twice. The clouds are building over the bay, the air thick, heavy with rain. Our clothes are sweat-soaked within blocks.

Chesty seems not to be bothered much by the heat or the humidity. But he's still in denial about the absence of attentive devotion from the people we pass. Well, not pass exactly. We're on the sidewalk, they've run out into the street. Ever the optimist, the dog continues to wag that tail in tight circles and prance at the approach of each woman, even as, again and again, they flee screaming. Now, who does that remind me of?

All right, I admit it, that was just plain mean. I told you I was in a bad mood. Not made any better by the humidity and big grin on the face of my husband. The phrase, "happy as if he had good sense," keeps running through my head on an endless loop.

Today we explore the El Cangrejo district as we walk. It's the same tree-lined streets as the financial district, but funkier, with more young people.

Passing a restaurant whose patio is scattered with smartly-dressed young couples sipping fruit drinks from tall glasses, Rocca decides she has found the perfect spot to void her bowels. I take the ever-present plastic bag from my pocket and slip it over my hand. This is a procedure that both dogs have practiced to perfection. Once she's finished her part of the job, Rocca goes as far away as the leash will allow from what is now my work, and sits and waits for me to clean up after her.

Once I've accomplished my goal and am holding a warm bag of dog shit, we go on our way. I sneak a look up at the lovely restaurant patio as we're walking away and see that our little performance has attracted the attention of many of the diners. What? They've never seen a woman holding a steaming bag of shit in one hand, the leash to a 148-pound dog in the other, tripping cluelessly along the sidewalks of their city looking for a garbage can?

It turns out there are no trash cans in this city. There are lovely, locked, wrought iron cages where restaurant workers and apartment dwellers deposit bags of trash for pick up by the local sanitation worker, but there are no public trash cans. Judging from the amount of garbage that is spilling from these decorative containers, the garbage collectors are on holiday this month along with the rest of the city.

By the time I catch up with Jack who, with Chesty, hasn't noticed that I am no longer walking directly behind him and is now two blocks ahead of me, I've lost patience with toting a bag of shit. I contribute Rocca's recycled dog food to the trash of an apartment building. Surreptitiously, I bring my hand up to my nose, just checking, and we continue with our jaunt. Having fulfilled the quest for a trash can in my own sneaky way, I am now in search of a public bathroom with a sink, hot water, and soap.

We discover a small, touristy, souvenir shop that has maps on display in the window. The aisles are much too narrow for pudgy *gringos* and two large dogs, so I hold both leashes while Jack goes inside to find us a good map. Of course, if the dogs misbehave, there is no way I'm going to be able to control both of them at the same time, but hopefully I'll be able to manage until Jack can rush out of the store and come to my aid.

Within a minute of Jack disappearing into the store, Chesty notices a crooked little man in a worn suit and a slightly lopsided Panama hat. The old gentleman is playing the violin. The instrument's case is open on the sidewalk, a few people stop and listen, drop a coin or two onto the faded, blue velvet interior. Chesty has seen many things in his working life. He's gone to the dentist, doctor, grocery store, and bank. But evidently, he's never seen an ancient, nearly toothless man playing the violin on a busy city street.

The dog's ears cock up and his muscles tense. I immediately give him a corrective snap of the leash and walk him away from his position with the old man in his direct line of sight. This could work, except that Rocca, who has discovered the cool tile of the shady store front, is stretched out on her belly. In the five seconds it takes her to lift her body off the ground, Chesty has progressed to full tail-wagging, bouncing interest in the musical entertainment. As I turn to walk away, Chesty crosses in front of me and Rocca, headed for the street musician.

I give him the strongest correction I can manage and turn again to walk in the opposite direction. My hope is to forcefully focus his attention on me by changing direction and surprising him just enough to break his concentration on the street performer. Unfortunately, both dogs are now tangled together, and I have one overly enthusiastic boy dog and one aggravated girl dog in a messy fur-and-slobber knot. Which is a complicated way of saying I am not in control of either dog.

In the two minutes it takes me to untangle the leads, separate the dogs, and get them walking away from the violin player, my adrenaline level is, more or less, at a cataclysmic level. My heart beats at the same rate it would if I ran four miles with a tiger chasing me. My breath is shallow and ragged, and I want to go home now. I'm not sure where home is, but I know it's someplace safe, and I want to go there. Also, my hand still smells like shit.

Jack remains in the store. I can see him through the glass store front. He has the same map in his hand that he had five minutes ago when I last looked. He's now examining ceramic frogs in Panama hats playing various musical instruments. He sees me watching him and holds up the frog with a set of bongo drums and gives me a big happy grin.

I give him a look that I'm hoping says, "You have one minute to pay for that map and get out here before I come in there, jerk that knick-knack out of your hand, and bludgeon you with a musical amphibian."

Ten minutes later, he's finished looking around and strolls out to join me and the dogs.

"You wanna go in the store now while I take the dogs? Check out the postcards—there's one of the Bridge of the Americas that's nice."

"Did you not see what *happened?*" I screech like a shrew.

"What?"

I hop up and down. Well, maybe not *physically* hop up and down, but verbally, emotionally—crazily—I hop up and down. I rant, and I rave and accomplish nothing but conveying to my husband that I am out of control.

"It seems like you handled it okay," Jack says. "Both dogs and you are safe and sound. Why are you getting so upset?"

I may be safe, but it's a raging lie that I am sound. I do, however, realize that I can't win this argument. Not here. Not now. Also, it's possible that Jack's correct and I am over-reacting. The problem is, I can't seem to stop. We go on back to the hotel without speaking, where we discover that the room is being cleaned.

Jack talks with the two young men doing the sweeping and cleaning while I sit on the couch and try to take deep breaths. Both dogs are still on their leads, and the two young workers are fascinated and frightened by them. Jack tries to convince them to touch Chesty, who is round-eyed and eager for the attention. Rocca lies on my feet, looks up at me, no doubt wonders why I'm making those little choking sounds.

Eventually the workers leave without having touched Chesty. I change into my pajamas and crawl into bed where I pull the covers up over my head and wonder if a person's heart really can leap out of her chest.

"Don't you want to go to lunch?" Jack asks. "I thought we'd try the restaurant downstairs. It's Italian."

Jack does not like Italian food, so this is a big concession for him. He's trying his best to help me. Maybe I'm a little bit appeased. Or maybe not.

"I'm not leaving this room with these dogs right now," I say from under the covers.

"Okay. Well. I'm going to get something to eat. You want me to bring you something?"

"I don't know."

"I'm going, then. See you when I get back. Do you want me to go ahead and take Chesty?"

"No!" Leave the dogs here where it's safe. Don't take them outside into the danger.

I can hear Jack singing outside the room as he walks down the hall to the elevator. "If ever I should leave you, it might be in spring time. Seeing you in spring time, I might just walk away."

He's nothing if not subtle, that man. I get up and look at the new map. Maybe planning the trip to Bocas will get my mind off the dogs. I spread the new map out next to the old one on the table and discover Jack's bought the exact same map we already have. It even has the same green-winged macaw on the cover. The same map that shows only one way to the islands. The one that shows what looks like a day-long trip up and around and over the mountains, dropping down, eventually, to the Caribbean. Huh. There's gotta be roads connecting those big stretches of the country. Doesn't there?

I've calmed down some by the time Jack comes back to the room with an individual-sized combination pizza, a six-pack of Diet Coke, and assorted candy bars.

"I'm sorry I'm getting so upset," I say in between bites of really-good pizza.

"Yeah. You need to stop it. I'm the crazy one in this marriage. If you go all nuts, we're in real trouble."

I think about this as I finish the entire pizza and three candy bars. We stretch out in the bed.

Just before we fall asleep, Jack says, "I talked to the hotel manager. There are only two ways to Bocas. Fly, which we can't do until probably December, or drive. The manager says they can arrange a taxi to take us."

"So, there's a different road than the one on our map? By the way, you bought the same exact map."

"Really? I wondered why it looked familiar. The girl said it was the best map of Panama."

"Huh," I say as we lay side by side, not touching, and fall into sleep.

We wake to discover that Rocca looked at the maps while we slept. She's eaten the Darién and Chiriquí provinces from one and the Panama City and Coclé regions of the other. So, no problem, we have a full map if we put them together, and don't mind the dog slobber and the teeth marks and the wrinkles. Really, we don't need a map anyway. We'll just tell the taxi driver where we want to go. Right?

EIGHT
WRESTLING ON THE ABYSS

J ACK HAS A degree in psychology, and he worked ten years counseling combat veterans from three wars and a couple of police actions. As I mentioned, he's a Vietnam combat Marine. He's not a right or wrong, good or bad, black or white kind of a guy.

"Does it make you happy?"

"Is it healthy for you to do that?"

"What have you learned from this experience?"

"What will be the consequences of that behavior?"

These are the foundations upon which he bases his actions, the questions he asks himself. Or so he claims. I suspect the actual question he asks himself is, "Do I, right this minute, want to do it?" If the answer is yes, and it always is or why would he be asking himself the question to begin with, he simply damns the consequences and goes full-speed ahead. To paraphrase James Lee Burke, Jack has only two speeds—full throttle and fuck it.

In addition, my husband feels he is more highly evolved than I because he does not factor into his calculations anything other than verbal communication. Okay. Maybe he doesn't feel like he's higher up the food chain exactly, but his unspoken body-language and tone of voice certainly lead me to draw that conclusion. A raised eyebrow, a shrug of the shoulder, a slight tilt of the head—all the minutiae of communication I find infinitely interesting—Jack never sees. Denies that he uses these cues and insists that other people tell him straight up what they expect from him, instead of expecting him to read and understand feelings from their crossed arms, tapping foot, and flashing eyes.

This male/female, yin/yang, right side/left side dialectic causes all the usual miscommunications in our marriage as it does in pretty much every other heterosexual relationship on the face of the planet. Jack has eight years of training in psychology. I, on the other hand, find that Jeff Foxworthy sums it up nicely when he lets women in on the secret of what men really want.

"Men want a beer, and they wanna see something naked. That's it, ladies. That's as complicated as it gets."

So, I do my best to be direct with Jack. I understand that, with my best friend, or with my mom or sister, I can communicate on six different levels at once. But not with my husband. Here's an example of the difference.

"How are you doing this morning?" he asks.

"Okay, I guess."

A simple little exchange, right?

To a man, yeah.

To a woman? Probably not.

If I have this conversation with Jack, he's going to follow-up with, "Well, good. Glad to hear it."

The same response of, "Okay, I guess" said to a woman is going to elicit, "What's wrong?" A woman is going to hear that mediocre, "Okay," followed by that obvious cry for help, "I guess," and she's going to know what I really said was, "I'm not doing well, and I'll tell you all about it if you love me enough to inquire further."

While it may appear that Jack and I are usually skipping happily over the rocks and crevasses and having ourselves a gay ol' time, picnic basket swinging between us, in truth there are clear rules and sign posts. Usually, either we decipher these sign posts in the same way, or we follow Jack's lead. But not always. Occasionally we wrestle around on the rocks and risk life-stealing plunges into the bone-crushing abyss before finally doing what Jack wanted to do all along.

You understand that, if you talk to Jack, he's going to tell you we always do things my way, he has no control issues whatsoever, and by the way, I hope you put cold beer in that picnic basket and are planning on getting naked when we get to where we're going.

All marriages have rules. Most of them are unspoken. One of our rules is that if I behave in a manner that is loony tunes, nutso, wacko—if you must be PC, you can substitute "unproductive" for these more colorful terms— Jack is going to respond by ignoring that behavior. He provides positive reinforcement for the behavior of which he approves and no reaction at all to those actions which he doesn't like. This works really well in a client/ counselor environment. In my experience, it is less productive or appropriate in a marriage.

Which is why I've been known to scream like an enraged banshee, "I'm not your fucking patient! I'm your freaking wife!"

To which his response is, you guessed it—nothing. Unless I happen to be naked with a cold beer clutched in my white-knuckled hand, and then the response, while it may be fun and all, isn't going resolve any burning issues for me.

Since I've been married to Jack, I've done many things that I never thought I was capable of doing. When I met him, I was afraid of heights, water, and close spaces. Today, I'm still afraid of those things from time to time, but I've learned to go through the fear and do it anyway.

"You don't have to like it. You just have to do it." This is the Marine Corps mantra that my husband repeated to me so many times over the years, it's now tattooed onto my psyche with the black ink of resignation.

Those are the words that have allowed me to cross suspension bridges in Nepal and thus see jungles and waterfalls and sights I would not have been able to experience without overcoming the fear. I've traversed tight caves and wiggle-room-only caverns in Vietnam to view giant, ancient Buddhas carved from the marble of the mountain itself. I've learned to scuba dive, opening up a fantastic world of colors and animals and fish, all of which I'd have missed out on if I hadn't "just done it."

When I learned to scuba dive, I was terrified of the water. I was never afraid of anything in the water. Curious sharks, graceful rays, conch- crunching loggerhead turtles—all these I loved. It was the water itself that sent me into a splashing, screaming, land-loving panic. This phobia seemed perfectly normal to me. Humans can't breathe down there!

"Ah," said Jack, "but we can. That's why we have a tank of air on our backs and a regulator in our mouths."

"Yes," I would bawl. "But a million things can happen to that equipment, which will lead me to die in that watery grave!"

"No," Jack would maintain. "Things can happen to the equipment, but nothing will make you die down there except your own panic."

Of course he was right, and I did, eventually, and very slowly with tiny, little steps, learn to love diving. It became my passion, my obsession. But occasionally, when I was feeling insecure on land, I would have a panic attack as I fell backwards off the boat and disappeared below the surface of the water. Here's how Jack handled my panic on those occasions.

He ignored it and went right on with his dive.

"Is there a problem with your equipment?"

"No!" I would shrill, splashing on the surface and managing to swallow a mouthful or two of salt water.

"Then what are you afraid of?" he would ask in that calm tone of voice that made me want to reach out and drown him.

"The water! I'm afraid of the water," I'd yell over to where he rested on the surface, safely out of my reach.

"Well, I'm sure you'll deal with that," he'd say as he disappeared below the waves.

I was never sure if, at those times, I actually overcame my fear or if my anger was stronger than my panic, and I had to catch him before I could take my little, pink-handled dive knife and stab him repeatedly until that calm, patronizing voice was silenced once and for all. When I caught up with him underwater, he would grin and yell a greeting through his regulator and do a fish-mating ballet dance around me in the water, and I'd remember why I probably shouldn't unsheathe my knife.

My point is that the patterns of behavior, which have worked, more or less, swell for the first fifteen years of our marriage, aren't working that great now that we're in a foreign country, looking for a home while dragging two pony-sized dogs around with us. The reason they aren't working has nothing to do with Jack. He is reacting the exact same way he always does. He's ignoring the negative and rewarding the positive. As defined, of course, by him.

The difference is me. And I have no idea what to do about it, and that is scaring the bejesus out of me, Jack, and both dogs. Chesty thinks I'll feel better if I just roll around on the floor with him and wrestle for the sock or hat or shirt that he's stolen and is now dangling from his grinning dog face, just out of my reach. Rocca has no idea what the problem is, but she feels that if she never leaves my side or stops licking me, I'll surely feel better before all my skin has been worn off. Jack thinks I'll feel ever so much better if I just fetch him a cold one and get naked.

NINE
INSIDE THE STORM, WITH CATS AND FLYING DEBRIS

THE BEST WIRELESS connection is from the roof of our hotel. Most afternoons, we take the elevator up to the covered patio after lunch. I sling the laptop over my shoulder. Rocca trudges with me. Chesty and Jack prance along beside us as happy as if they had good sense.

Once on the roof, I email friends. Then, in a fit of homesickness, I Skype. Those conversations go something like this:

"Hello."

"Hi! Can you hear me?" I scream.

"Hello?"

"Can you hear me?" Struggling not to cry, my voice pitches high enough that only dogs can hear.

"Is somebody there?"

"It's me. Pam. I'm calling from the roof of the hotel in Panama. Can you hear me?"

"Hello? Is anybody there?"

"I guess you can't hear me. I love you. I'll call back later."

"Hello?"

After which Jack invariably says, "Now. Don't you feel better having talked to your mom?"

Or Mona. Or your sister. Or your boys. Depending on who I have just subjected to intercountry communication by computer phone.

Occasionally, we do get a connection that allows a few minutes of conversation. Unfortunately, the communication usually breaks up at the worst possible time. Like in the middle of me finally getting past pretending that everything is just hunky-dory-peachy-keen and actually confessing my fears. I can always hear the other person, even when they can't hear me, as though I'm dead and desperately seeking to communicate with my living loved ones. I do learn in this way that my mother knows a lot more cuss words than I ever suspected.

The wonderful thing about these afternoon rooftop excursions is the storms. They roll in across the ocean, slowly obscuring the skyscrapers that line the crescent bay of the city. Here on the eighth floor, we're actually inside the black clouds and hard rain. Chesty jumps up and puts his front feet on the three-foot railing and barks back at the booming thunder. Rocca growls and pushes herself tighter against my side. Jack and I hold hands and kiss.

Maybe coming to Panama wasn't such a terrible idea.

The show occurs like clockwork at 2:00 p.m. every day. This magnificent, powerful display of nature becomes my church, my communication with my higher power, my adrenaline rush, my sanctuary, my Prozac, my lifeline. These are the moments when I forget that I am metaphorically drinking my own urine.

Over the next several days, we make our plans to get to Bocas del Toro. Traveling by plane is out. All flights are booked for the next three weeks. Okay. No problem. We'll rent a car and drive over. Well, there's a glitch with that idea too. A number of snags actually.

First of all, car rentals here are very cheap. We were clever and checked that out on the internet before we came down. However, insurance on rental cars is expensive. More than the cost of the car rental. And since we no longer have a vehicle in the United States, we no longer have insurance that will just slide over and protect us on a rental.

Huh. Okay, well, no need to panic. That makes the idea expensive but not impossible. We could bite the bullet and pay for the rental car and insurance. Every day in the city is costing us money paying for the hotel and food.

CLUELESS GRINGOS IN PARADISE 63

But no. There's another little speed bump in the road of this plan. There are only two places in the country where rental cars can be picked up and returned. Panama City and the city of David. David is a ten-hour drive from Almirante, which is the town on the mainland where we would get on the ferry to go to the islands. So how do we return the car after we get there?

We could leave the car at Almirante, go to the islands and find a hotel, and then Jack could come back on the ferry, drive the car to David, take the bus back to Almirante and a boat to join me in the hotel room on Bocas. This is a workable plan if the car is actually still in the unsecured lot when he returns for it. Certainly, he'll have no trouble finding me once he gets to the islands after his two-or-three-or-four-day, lone adventure. He can just follow the crazed howls.

"If the dogs didn't rush out doors," I say, "if they came back when they were called, on even an occasional basis, then I could stay three or four days and nights in a hotel with them, and we'd all be alive and sane when you got back. But, the way the dogs are… no. I can't handle both dogs. I'm not doing it."

"I don't know when you became so cautious." Jack shakes his head at me.

"Somewhere on the flight down here, between the time I realized the dogs would be lying under our feet and on top of each other for the entire trip and when Rocca jumped Chesty in the Houston airport. Right in that time frame is when I lost my nerve."

Big non-verbal communication—a heavy sigh and head shake of exasperation from my husband.

"I'm sorry, Jack, but I can't do it. I cannot control both of these dogs."

"I didn't say anything. Did I say anything?"

Jack takes Chesty and leaves to go downstairs and see what else he can figure out.

He flees from his biggest irritation, goes off in search of a solution that will satisfy his frightened wife. His sonorous tones Doppler down the breezeway with, "Nobody knows the trouble I've seen. Nobody knows my problems." An hour later, I hear him belting out, "She's sixteen, she's beautiful, and she's cheap," as he makes his way back to me with another suggestion.

"The manager here says we can hire a taxi to take us to Bocas for the same price we can rent a car."

"The price with or without insurance?"

"Oh. I don't know. Without, I think. It's her cousin."

"The young, good-looking *chica* who works behind the desk? The one who had her picture taken with you and Chesty?"

"Is she good-looking? I didn't notice," he says with an absolutely straight face.

From me, he gets the powerful, nonverbal communication of the well-documented, wife truth-eliciting-stare.

"Okay," he grins, "I noticed. She's got really nice boobs, too."

"Ah... yeah. So. The cousin taxi driver guy? He knows about the dogs?"

"Yeah, yeah, yeah. He's seen 'em. He has no problem with the dogs."

This is said with emphasis on "he" and a tone of voice that clearly means, "unlike my chicken-shit wife, who seems to be obsessing over problems about the dogs."

"Okay. What kind of car does he have?"

"I haven't seen it, but it's a big SUV with plenty of room for the dogs, us, and our luggage."

"All right. When do we leave?"

"Day after tomorrow. It's all set."

"Do we have hotel reservations for us *and the dogs* when we get to Bocas?"

"No. But I'm sure that won't be a problem."

I admit it. I screech a little right about here.

"Just you saying 'it won't be a problem,' doesn't mean it won't be a problem. I'm not going without hotel reservations at a place where they know about the dogs. I'm not going to sleep on the beach with our giant dogs because we can't get a room."

"I'll find us a room when we get there. Why do you have to make everything so complicated?"

"I'm not *making* it complicated! It *is* fucking complicated!"

Another monstrous sigh of frustration from my husband, another heave of the shoulders.

"I'm sorry," I say, using my inside voice once again. "You did good to get the taxi set up. I just think we should do everything we can to make sure things go as smoothly as possible, because having Chesty and Rocca with us is unusual, and people aren't used to dealing with two big dogs."

"You don't trust me to make sure they're safe?"

No, I do not.

"Of course I trust you. It's not that. I just think you have a higher tolerance for inconvenience than I do right now."

We leave it at that and take the dogs for a walk. On the way past the lobby desk, the cutie behind the counter gives Jack one of those little finger-wiggling waves, ducks her head, and winks. He probably really needs the attention right now, traveling as he is with his unreasonable shrew of a wife.

His voice booms into the lobby, startling the sweat-soaked couple checking-in and bringing a wide grin to the face of the doorman. "She's sixteen, she's beautiful, and she's hot."

This late afternoon walk is completed with nothing more challenging than a couple of cats helping themselves at the garbage boxes. We've learned by now that it's easier if we don't walk the two dogs close to each other. Chesty shows off his macho protectiveness for Rocca, and Rocca, who must always be the boss, insists on outdoing him by killing whatever he's found that entertains him.

Separately, an encounter with a stray cat goes something like this:

Chesty barks, *"Hey! Hey! Hey! A cat! A cat! Can I chase it? Can I? Can I?"*

Jack gives a tiny correction with the leash, telling him, "No! No cat-chasing while you're working."

Chesty asks, *"Really? Are you sure? I could catch it really fast. It'd hardly take a minute."*

Another small snap of the leash and Chesty gives a doggie sigh and prances right past the cat with only a look that says, *If I didn't have this big galoot at the other end of this leash, you and I, Sylvester, would have us a good ol' time.*

Rocca feels that cats are so far below her that she doesn't even bother to look at them—when she's away from Chesty.

When the two of them are together, the same meeting goes something like this:

Chesty barks, *"Hey! Hey! A cat! Watch me, Rocca! Are you watching? Huh? Huh? Are you?"*

Jack gives a correction on the leash and a firm, "No!"

Chesty, still looking over his shoulder at his girl, insists, *"I can catch him! I can. Watch me! Watch me now."*

By this time, Chesty has Rocca's full attention, and she's caught up in the event unfolding on the busy city sidewalk with literally tons of fast-moving vehicles whizzing past. She joins in, *"Get that cat, Big Boy! Show me what you can do."*

This pretty much seals the deal for Chesty, and he ends up being dragged away from the cat while he lunges and barks and acts like a typical male making a fool of himself while showing off for a female. Rocca, watching all this, now has enough adrenalin roaring through her system that she's developed her own plan for the cat. She walks up to where it's now hissing and spitting, humped up in a little furry arch of fear and sharp claws. She feigns no interest in the cat whatsoever. When she comes alongside, she suddenly leaps, 148 pounds of adrenaline-enhanced estrogen, in an attempt to eat the damn cat in one bite.

I much prefer the scenario where they behave like actual working dogs while trying to exercise them along sidewalks with large openings into flowing drainage water, constantly honking horns, and pedestrians fleeing from us. So, Jack and I now walk the dogs about a block apart. Which, given how frustrated we are with each other right now, is probably a good thing, don't ya think?

TEN

WORRY AND FRET, BITE MY TONGUE, AND THE SCREECHING OF A GIANT MOUSE

TIRED OF LISTENING to me worry that we are going to be sleeping on the beach at Bocas where we will undoubtedly be beaten and robbed by locals, recovering in the hospital just in time to come down with the malaria we've contracted from 25,000 mosquito bites while the dogs earn a name for themselves in the dog fight arena, Jack decides to go ahead and get hotel reservations for the islands before we leave in the morning. You're probably wondering why, if I'm so Goddamn worried about the reservation, I don't just go downstairs, bat my eyelashes at the night manager, and make the arrangements myself.

If this is indeed your thought process, you still have not grasped the division of labor in my marriage. I can no more take charge than the male lion can trot out and kill his own dinner while the lionesses lie in the shade and lick their paws. On the rare occasions when I travel alone, I'm perfectly capable of making arrangements. But when Jack's on the trip, he makes all the decisions. This is partly because he needs to be in control and partly because, over the years, I have gotten lazy. But mostly it's because this is just how we do things. So, I worry and fret, wring my hands, and cry. He gets annoyed and then does what I want him to do. Except it's rarely the way I want it done.

I didn't say it was a good system. I just said that's the way we do things.

The second reason Jack is making all the arrangements on this particular little adventure is that it's all I can do just to walk the dogs, go out to eat with the dogs, and do a minimal amount of exploring around the city while keeping the shaking and twitching and crying to a manageable level. I'm a wreck, and both Jack and I are already good and sick of it.

While he's downstairs making the reservations, the dogs and I enjoy the air conditioning and watch some TV. Some of the programs are in English, but all the commercials are in Spanish. If the advertising is to be believed, every man and every woman in the country gets up each morning and bathes in expensive perfume, after which they float out into the city causing traffic accidents and having peculiar encounters on elevators with strangers. I've never seen so many perfume advertisements. And I haven't smelled a drop of so much as toilet water cologne since we landed.

Jack comes back upstairs with a slight change of plans. There are about a dozen motels on the island of Colón, which is the main island of Bocas del Toro. All of the motel managers laughed when asked for a room for two people traveling with two dogs. But Jack has persevered and found us a room at the Hotelito del Mar.

Eight days from now.

"I talked to the manager, and she said it would be no problem with the dogs, but she doesn't have a room until next Tuesday," he tells me.

I do not say out loud that, if I hadn't insisted on the reservation, we really would have been sleeping on the beach.

He reads my mind. Not that difficult, even for Jack. "We'd have found something if we had just shown up with the dogs. But this way, we'll stay here for another week at sixty-five dollars a night so you don't have to worry about having a room when we get there."

"Thank you." It's all I can manage without biting off the tip of my tongue.

———

SINCE WE'RE STUCK in the city for another week, we do a little exploring. With the dogs. Panama City's skyline is impressive. The only city I've ever been in with this many skyscrapers is New York. Even San Francisco doesn't boast this many. Bangkok and some of the other

Asian capitals where space is at a premium may have more per square mile, but what makes these Panama buildings beautiful is that they are spread out along the circle of the bay. At night, they create a sparkling jeweled rim along the deep curve of the ocean. Many of the high-rises have distinctive shapes and designs lending a rich look of opulence to the view. The city seems to shout, "Money! Wealth! Conspicuous consumption!" It's all very impressive for this redneck girl from rural America.

The other distinctive construction that Panama City boasts is the canal and the Bridge of the Americas which spans it. It is visible from many parts of the city. Day or night, the sight of the ships lined up at the mouth of the canal with the bridge in the background is beautiful, exciting, and exotic. Because of the canal, Panama has virgin rainforests minutes away from the city. The builders of the passageway understood that cutting that rainforest would cause erosion and endanger the hard-earned passage, so a five-mile area on either side of the zone has been protected all these years. Because of this, all this man-made beauty of skyscrapers and bridges is backdropped by dense, in some cases, triple canopy jungle where monkeys and sloths, parrots and harpy eagles still live and flourish.

I would like to tell you that I enjoy all of this and let myself be caught up in the excitement of seeing such an exotic and beautiful place. But I'd be lying. The city is filled with sights and sounds that penetrate my anxiety, but only as brief glimpses of another reality, as a dream will register in your conscious mind for those first few cloudy moments of waking. Mostly, I worry about the safety of the dogs. And drive Jack insane doing it.

Jack arrives in the room after a morning trip downstairs to walk Chesty and announces, "Get up and have your coffee. We're leaving in an hour to see Casco Viejo."

I know from the Lonely Planet guide book that this is an older section of the city. The only thing I remember about the area is the warning *Do not walk here at night.*

"Well," says Jack reasonably enough, "it's not night is it? And we have two big dogs who will protect us from anyone."

True. The question is, can I protect the dogs from anything?

It's useless to argue. It will only burn up energy I'm going to need for this jaunt. So I drink my coffee, get dressed, and we go downstairs to see about getting to Casco Viejo. Jack now knows all the taxi drivers and the vendors within a five-block area of the hotel. They call to him as we come out of the hotel doors. They also call out to Chesty, who twirls his tail around and prances along in princely style. Rocca and I look much less royal. I already have sweat running down my back, and Rocca is panting in the fashion of all big-boned girls.

The taxi Jack has commissioned for us is driven by a young man whose name is Guillermo.

"*En Inglés soy* Bill," he tells us, and I smile because I might just be able to remember that.

Bill leads us to his chariot—a typical local taxi. There are shiny new cabs in the city. Lots of them. But, funny thing, we haven't yet encountered a driver of such a prize who will allow us inside with the dogs. Not for any amount of money. Bill's vehicle is younger than me, but not by much. I doubt it has more than 350,000 miles on it, and I'm positive it's been in no less than a dozen minor accidents and outright wrecks. It's a four-door sedan of mostly a dark, faded blue color. The hood is red, one back section of the passenger side is gray. But, mostly it's blue.

So, with Jack beaming and Bill talking non-stop in Spanish, we climb in the car. Jack's in the front seat with Chesty on his lap. I'm in the back seat with Rocca beside me. The front seat is fixed in one permanent position, a sort of three-quarters recline that would be fine if you wanted to take a snooze and didn't have a 110-pound dog on your chest.

"Ha, ha, ha," says Jack as he settles inside with Chesty hanging his head out the open window.

"*Esta bien, no? Muchas brisas.*" It's good, right? A lot of fresh air.

From this I conclude that the window doesn't actually go up. A closer inspection shows that there is no window glass at all.

Bill attempts to start the engine with a pair of needle-nosed pliers, and when that doesn't do the trick, he calls on a friend to help him by doing something with a hammer under the hood. That done, the engine coughs to struggling life and off we go. I am now worried that when this taxi breaks down—and it will, of that I have no doubt—we will be left to find our way back to the hotel on our own as no other taxi will take us with the dogs.

Something you should know about taxis in Panama City. They are regulated and very cheap. But, because their fees are restricted and because all taxi drivers in this city evidently have been sired by German engineers, they never go anywhere in a straight line. The drivers do their best to avoid the traffic jams that plague the city. They do this by going around their elbow to get to their ass. They avoid main streets and police wherever possible.

So, having looked at the map before we left (Rocca did leave most of Panama City intact), I think I know how we'll get to Casco Viejo from the hotel. Our buddy Bill is going in the complete opposite direction. Near as I can tell. Certainly, we are not headed toward the bay which is where we're supposed to end up. I would like to mention this to Jack, but he's in the front seat and deep in conversation with Guillermo.

Chesty has his head out the window, his tongue flapping out the side of his mouth as he grins at everyone we pass. I'm hoping that enough people will remember seeing the dog that the police will eventually recover our bodies. Because we are not headed for Casco Viejo. No way.

We are being driven into one of those areas of the city with back-to-back high-rise apartment buildings built about the same time as the car in which we're riding to our death.

Another thing about Panama City is that there are almost no street signs, and except for the main drags, the streets are narrow, as though designed to accommodate an ox cart of Spanish gold. Along these streets, which are really narrow tunnels through overhanging flowering trees, people park their vehicles on both sides. Usually they are considerate and pull all four wheels up on the sidewalk. This leaves enough room for one car to work its way carefully along.

The streets are two-way, and the definition of working your way along a narrow street in this city is to speed along blowing your horn and to never, ever give ground. It's a game of chicken. The biggest vehicle has the right of way. Except when the bigger vehicle is new, usually an SUV, or the other vehicle is a taxi. Taxi drivers are the kamikazes of Panama. Everybody backs down for a taxi. We hope. Because God knows, our pal Bill isn't giving any ground.

The taxi turns down an alley between moldy cement apartments and Bill says something in Spanish. The only word I understand is "*amigo.*" I assume he's going to get his friend to help butcher us and steal the dogs. I'd mention this possibility to Jack, but he has his hands full controlling Chesty who has spotted a Rottweiler on a balcony above us.

It's the usual, *"Bark! Bark! Bark! Come down here and say that!"*

"Woof! Woof! If I weren't chained here on this balcony, I'd come down there and kick your furry ass!"

Jack lets Chesty bark and attempt to force his body out the window. I suppose he identifies with the need to posture and make threatening noises. I was given instruction before we left the hotel room. I've been told to watch Rocca and not worry about Chesty who is, at this moment, hanging well over half-way out of the car. I emit little screeching noises that sound similar to a giant mouse caught in a trap, which are not audible over Chesty's barking and achieve nothing except to allow me to release tiny bursts of my anxiety.

Rocca, like the old Popeye of cartoon fame loses patience before I do. She explodes with, *"That's all I can stands. I can't stands no more!"*

She leaps across the seat and into the middle of Chesty. Who, you will recall, has his back legs on Jack's chest and his entire front half out the window. Rocca's action produces a five-second dog fight in the middle of Jack's lap during which, judging by his bellowing, at least one dog manages to put a foot down on a vulnerable part of Jack's body.

Jack is still recovering when here comes our buddy Bill with four raggedy friends, all wearing huge grins. None are packing machetes, and I take this as a good sign. As near as I can figure, we have stopped here in this scenic ghetto spot because our driver knows that, unless they see it for themselves, his *amigos* are not going to believe his story of the two crazy *gringos* who are staying in a high-rise hotel in the city with two dogs as big as ponies and who he is personally escorting around the city in his taxi. We climb out of the car and meet some friendly locals.

The four of us, two humans and two dogs, arrange ourselves instinctively in the muddy alley back-to-back, each of us facing a different point on the compass. Chesty and Jack both have the same big, confident grins on their faces, though Jack's tongue isn't hanging sideways from the side of his face like his cohort's. I'm wearing a somewhat forced smile, and my sweet Rocca girl is doing her active volcano impersonation and sending out earthshaking rumbles from deep in her belly. None of the large, grinning gentlemen try to steal the dogs or chop us into manageable pieces though the whole episode. Makes me think we should begin calling this relocation experience, "Clueless Gringos in Paradise."

ELEVEN
A PATINA OF MOLD, AN ARMY OF CATS, AND THE RUSTY BLADE OF A KNIFE

CASCO VIEJO IS beautiful, rundown, dirty, and impressive as hell. It's the only place in Panama we've seen yet that is colonial in architecture. The buildings have thick cement walls that look as though they were built to repel cannonballs. In fact, some of these jagged holes may actually be from cannonballs. A patina of age and salt and dirt makes everything slimy to the touch and slightly putrid to the nose. An occasional building is in the process of being restored. Gentrification is inching its moneyed nose in the moldy door here, but it's creeping forward at a sloth's pace. Mostly, the neighborhood looks like a place where people who can't afford to live anywhere else squat in abandoned buildings and make a living by ambushing the occasional tourist stupid enough to enter the area unprepared.

Paseo de Las Bóvedas is a walkway that runs along the top of the protective seawall built by the Spanish. Kuna and Emberá Indians have colorful blankets and old plastic tarps laid out here with their mola quilts, beaded bracelets, baskets, and painted feathers displayed for sale. Walking along the wall, we look across the bay at ships lined up, waiting for their turn to enter the locks.

The Panama Canal! Wow!

Standing on the seawall, on the dark, slippery cobblestones, we gape at a skyline to rival any in the world. A modern, growing city, rich in resources and technology, back-to-back with a part of the country's history that is falling away, one mold-blackened cement wall at a time.

Coming away from the bay, we discover the streets in Casco Viejo are dark, narrow alleys with two- and three-story buildings on each side with front doors opening directly to the road. We thread our way along cobblestoned paths, narrow balconies on the upper floors cantilevered just above our heads. If I raise my hand over my head, I can touch the dripping bottoms of these overhangs.

Colorful people wander through these dark alleys, going about the business of living. These individuals are almost exclusively poor or old, or handicapped by physical or mental disabilities or substance abuse. Everyone seems friendly enough. At no time do I feel threatened by them.

The threat here is from the ten thousand stray cats that live in the area.

These *gatos* linger in shadowy doorways, hiss and growl from garbage bins, appear from under benches and bushes in roving attack groups. I walk Rocca a block ahead in the hope that Chesty won't feel the need to show off for his lady, but I can hear Jack's attempt to control his dog.

"Bark bark bark! Can I get'em, Dad? Please, please, can I?"

"No!"

"How 'bout this one? He looks like he needs to die. Can I get him, huh?"

"No!"

"An army of cats! These I gotta chase! Come on Dad, it'll be fun. Did you hear what that one said to me? I'm gonna kill him. Let me! Let me!"

"God damn it, I said NO!"

And so on and so forth. Three or four hundred times. Around every corner, behind every broken curb. And these aren't the domestic kind of cats that run away in fright from a dog. These little buggers live here. They own this neighborhood. This is the equivalent of a Blood walking through Crip territory. Well, if the Crips had nothing to defend with but tiny, little razor-sharp knives and the Blood had a machine gun.

I mentioned earlier that the local people seem to view every large dog as though it is going to run them to ground and feast on their flesh. Well, Chesty's barking and lunging and general excitement over the cats is doing nothing to alleviate the anxiety of the locals today. The fact that everything is crowded together on narrow cobblestone lanes with nowhere to walk around us as we stroll along with our two giant dogs also ratchets up the level of anxiety significantly.

I am ready to leave as soon as we encounter the second cat, but we've told the taxi driver, good ol' Guillermo, to return in two hours. Of course, because I am taking a crash course in worrying about every single friggin' thing that could possibly go wrong, I assume our buddy Bill either isn't going to show up at all, or he's going to show up with a dozen or so guys from this neighborhood to steal the dogs, our passports, and money, after which we will end up as fish and cat food.

About the time we pass the hundredth cat, I begin to think that the greater danger is that Chesty will break away from Jack, and we are going to be arrested after the dog creates havoc chasing cats through these dark alleys and abandoned buildings. If I could get close enough to Jack without Chesty showing off for Rocca and Rocca getting her leash in a knot as she too catches cat fever, I know Jack would assure me that he has Chesty under control at all times. However, judging by how all two dozen policemen on this beat now seem to be following us from one tiny alley to the next, I'm not sure that's apparent to anyone but Jack.

Also, I understand that a police presence is supposed to reassure visitors of the safety of the area. However, men with automatic rifles slung over their shoulders are not a comfort to me. And these guys aren't smiling. In fact, Jack is doing his usual thing with his big grin and stumbling Spanish and booming laugh, yet none of these brown-shirted, armed gentlemen appear to be in any way appeased. These boys are locked, loaded, and looking for prey.

We find a small, filthy luncheonette where there don't appear to be any cats. Before we even step into the greasy place, four cops inform us that we cannot take the dogs inside. This is perfectly reasonable, but it still pisses me off. We continue walking the cat gauntlet while I mutter about how just last week we had both dogs in Red Lobster in Tucson, and no one said a word. Of course, the staff at that seafood restaurant didn't have any choice as United States law requires them to allow service dogs inside. There's also the little difference that, at the time we entered the Red Lobster, both dogs were not behaving like cat-crazed lunatics. I understand all this, but I need to be mad at someone, and the police are a good target.

By the time the taxi returns, my mood has deteriorated to around that metaphorical level where I'm about to make my first attempt to hack off my good, strong hand with a rusty Swiss Army knife. Guillermo is a happy sight to see, standing by his beater taxi with a wide grin on his face. On the ride to the hotel, a loose spring stabs me in the butt each time the shock absorber-less vehicle hits one of the two or three hundred bumps along the way. Doesn't matter. We make it back safe and as sound as can be expected. I collapse in a heap in bed and pull the covers up over my head.

"Where would you like to go to lunch?" Jack asks innocently enough.

I pull the sheet down, expose one evil eye.

"I'm not leaving this room again with these dogs."

"Until when?"

"Maybe not ever. I'm going to stay right here until we all die of starvation, and our swollen bodies are found by those nice young men who clean each day. We'll leave the air conditioner going, so the discovery won't traumatize them too much."

Ever practical and not amused, Jack says, "I'm going to lunch."

I hide my head and cry silently, piteously into the pillow.

The tears don't last long. Unfortunately, the twitching continues but I ignore it and try to think through the recent behavior of our wonderfully-trained service dogs. For one thing, they haven't been off-lead since we left our house in Arizona. These are dogs that have been raised on five acres where they had the run of the property. And they did run it. Every day they weren't out in public working with Jack, they ran the five prickly acres wearing paths around mesquite trees, creosote bushes, and cow's tongue cacti.

Rocca has never been as athletic as Chesty, nor does she have his prey drive. She learned early on to conserve her energy by using her size and her bark and growl to intimidate just about anything that might walk, crawl, or fly onto her property. Chesty, on the other hand, caught his first rabbit before he was six months old and his first jackrabbit at just over a year. He's big and fast and can turn on the proverbial dime.

We had a small corral on the property in Arizona that we had to put chicken wire around to protect our small garden from the hundreds of rabbits that lived there B.C.—Before Chesty. The dog would catch bunnies and trot with them, head high and proud, to the corral. He'd drop his catch at his feet and then paw at the unfortunate animal until the slobber-soggy thing built up enough courage to make a run for it. Chesty would quickly catch the poor rabbit again as it bounced off the chicken wire. He loved this game.

The cottontails usually died of a heart attack fairly quickly, but a jackrabbit is a long-legged, kicking, biting machine with a whole different attitude. Those generally lasted three or four minutes before Chesty crunched a little too enthusiastically on retrieval. He'd paw at the carcass for a few more minutes and then pick up his limp new friend and trot to us with it hanging from his mouth. Laying it at our feet, he'd whine and cry and paw at the carcass and look up at us as though saying, *"Make it play some more! How come my little friends never want to play with me for long?"*

Before we got Chesty, we had several bird feeders in the yard. I stopped feeding the birds after I watched him leap straight into the air and pluck a snacking bird from the feeder hanging five feet up on the branch of a spreading mesquite. These feathered friends he would also hold in his mouth, wanting to play. If we could get to him before one of his giant paws broke every bone in the poor little feathered thing's body, we could usually make a successful rescue. Jack would sit the drool-dripping bird on a high branch, I would bring Chesty in the house, and eventually the bird would work the slimy glue from its feathers and be on its way with a story to tell.

Now, with no yard to patrol, no rabbits to run down, no coyotes to guard against, Chesty is bursting with pent up energy. As much as I hate to think about it, we're going to have to walk him more. The only place we have to do that is here in the city, with the traffic and the crowded sidewalks and the occasional darting, garbage-eating cat.

Have I told you how to cross a busy street in Panama City? No? The first thing I do is mutter a Hail Mary.

"Pray for us sinners, now and at the hour of our death."

Death, which given the fact that pedestrians do *not* have the right of way, could be real damn soon. There are crosswalks, but they are more like straight lines designating the target at which the speeding vehicles aim. There are the occasional overhead walkways with fifty-two steps going up, a covered ramp over the busier streets, and another fifty-two steps going down. All this is in a narrow tunnel where anyone we meet with the dogs is going to give a squeal—ranging in loudness from frightened mouse squeak to bull moose roar—then cling to the side of the tunnel while we pass as though we own their friggin' country.

Mostly, the way we cross the streets here is to keep the dogs in a tight heel against our left leg and then step out into the flow of traffic. We make our way from lane to lane, standing in whatever space we can as the cars zip and roar past until we make it to the other side, and I complete the crossing with a second prayer. On busier streets, this is actually easier as the cars are often gridlocked, and we just weave our way between the stopped SUV's and old taxis. We've only been in the country five days, and we've heard three horror stories of people getting hit and killed while crossing a city street. I'm sure these stories are wildly exaggerated and repeated by people who only want to frighten us.

Good job.

As I'm thinking of all this and how, like it or not, we're going to have to brave the big bad city in order to get more exercise for the dogs, Jack comes back. He doesn't bring me anything to eat.

"If you're hungry, I'll stay with the dogs. You go out and get something."

Reasonable bastard!

I go to the Café Pomodoro, the restaurant in the hotel courtyard, and get a sandwich. A really good sandwich as it turns out. With salami and cheese and some kind of sauce I can't identify, which is delicious. A young couple is here having lunch with their two young children, a little girl and a slightly older brother. The ordinariness of the scene makes me miss my boys. They're big, grown up men now, but an eye blink ago they were the age of these two kids I'm watching as I munch my sandwich and wonder what in the hell I'm doing 5,000 quadrillion miles away from my own kids.

After lunch, I find Jack getting the dogs ready for their afternoon walk, which we begin just as the rains sweep in off the bay, drenching us within seconds. It hardly matters. We're dripping wet from the heat and humidity anyway. The rain just cools things off. The only complication is that the balconies overflow. No matter how careful we are, the backs of our shirts fill with the dirty runoff water. Also, my glasses immediately become fogged, so I'm walking blind. The good news is there aren't that many people on the sidewalks, and all the cats are in hiding.

This is pretty much how we pass the next five days until we leave for Bocas. We walk the dogs. I twitch and pray and shake. We go to the roof and email all our friends about the exotic and exciting adventure in which we've embarked. We lie a lot. We walk to the Rey Supermarket and buy Corvina, which is delicious sea bass, and cook it on the hot plate in the room. We go to restaurants, where Jack eats and I tremble and squeak and drink frothy cappuccino. We watch TV. We stare out at the skyline with the rain rushing across to engulf us each day at 2:00 p.m. We wait and hope things are going to get better for us. We imagine Bocas del Toro as a green sanctuary in the turquoise blue waters of a calm Caribbean Sea. We breathe and wait and think, and I wonder if I'm going to get this boulder of anxiety off me before it kills me dead.

TWELVE
MOUTHS OF THE BULL

THE 3:00 A.M. wake-up call pulls me out of the only ten minutes of sleep I've managed to find tonight. Time for the next leg of our journey. *Bocas del Toro.* Mouths of the Bull. Islands in the deep blue sea.

I pull on my jeans and shoes, wear the T-shirt in which I tossed and turned all night. Three minutes for my hair and teeth, and I'm as ready as I'm going to get. I stay in the room with both dogs in their service capes, on their leashes, looking at me as though I've lost what's left of my mind. Chesty sits, takes a last look around his high-rise home. Rocca lies at my feet and goes back to sleep.

"Wake me when this newest nonsense is over," seems to be her attitude.

Jack returns from stowing our luggage in the SUV taxi we've rented to take us the length and breadth of the country of Panama. He tells me our driver's name is Manuel. As if I care at the moment. One last ride in the glass elevator, during which Rocca doesn't even bother to flatten herself out, but merely hangs her head and gives a small groan of annoyance. Chesty is his usual prancing self. Jack has seemed a little subdued since coming back from loading the taxi, but this hasn't registered with me yet. I, like Rocca, am not really attuned to my environment at the moment. I am not a morning person. Especially without my coffee.

Parked at the door of the hotel is a battered, twelve-year-old Toyota hatchback. I'm still looking around for the SUV that will be our ride when Jack begins loading the dogs on top of the luggage, under the slanted glass top of the hatchback. Chesty is already in the vehicle. He slips on the luggage and does his best to find a comfortable place to stand. Jack has him lie down, and then he turns to me to load Rocca, who evidently is going to be making the twelve-hour trip lying on top of Chesty. If looks could kill, the one both Rocca and I give Jack would leave a pillar of hardened shit, standing for all eternity in the wet gutter in front of the Las Vegas Suites in Panama City.

"This is not going to work," I say.

"What? Of course it will. We're going. Just have your dog jump up and lie down. This is just like on the plane. No problem."

The back seat already holds two pieces of luggage, so there's no way either dog is going to fit there next to me, and I can't envision how they're going to wedge themselves in here.

"Jack! Honey. This isn't going to work. We're going to have to get a different car. I thought this was going to be an SUV."

Jack drops Chesty's lead and takes Rocca's leash from me. This shifts my attention from loading the dogs to preventing Chesty from spotting a cat and leaping free from his perch on top the luggage. I snag Chesty's leash while Jack instructs Rocca to load. Like an abused child who'll do anything for Daddy, she pulls her big body up so she's lying on top of two daypacks and half of Chesty. Chesty begins circling that stubby tail of his. His eyes are round and happy.

"Oh, boy. Are we goin' on an adventure, Dad? Are we? Huh? Huh?"

Rocca, thoroughly disgusted, merely groans and grunts and wiggles until she's as comfortable as she can make herself. Jack shuts the glass hatchback pressing both dogs down into the luggage. The dogs readjust so their heads aren't quite touching the glass, and Jack grins.

"See. No problem."

The night crew from the hotel are here to tell us goodbye, collect their tips, and see for themselves that we're actually going to fit in this vehicle. I wave *chao*. Jack gives away money and one more booming laugh. I climb in the back seat, Jack in the front, and off we go.

We make it less than a mile before both dogs crawl over the back seat, their big butts under glass and their giant heads on my shoulders. Jack asks Manuel to pull over, and he and I switch seats. On Jack's authority, the dogs slip back under glass and we continue on our way. In predawn dark, the city streets are free flowing. Crossing the Bridge of the Americas, I look down to see a dozen ships waiting their turn to cross to the Atlantic Ocean, their lights a ragged necklace on the Pacific's dark waters.

"Pretty impressive, huh?" Jack asks.

Well, yeah. It is. And if I could allow myself to feel anything from under this soggy, gray blanket of fear in which I've cloaked myself from the moment we actually left the hotel in this vehicle *with these two dogs,* I bet I'd really enjoy the experience. Deep, black exhaustion overtakes me before we're even completely across the bridge, and I float on the surface of sleep, seeing nothing of the countryside until the taxi slows, and we stop for gas and a cup of coffee almost three hours later.

To get out of the car safely with the dogs requires that I exit while Jack holds the leashes. The driver opens the hatch which, in theory, frees the dogs to stand and move a little. In reality, it takes them a moment or two to get the feeling back into their legs. Then I take the leashes from Jack, and Chesty leaps and Rocca lumbers out from the back of the car. We walk them around the parking area while the attendant fills the gas tank.

There's coffee here. I can smell it. We offer water to the dogs, but Chesty's too busy playing with his new pals—six national policemen with automatic rifles slung over their shoulders—and Rocca isn't interested in anything but grunting and groaning and letting me know what she thinks of this newest leg of our adventure.

We walk the dogs for ten minutes, gulp a cup of coffee, Jack gets the names and numbers of two of the police officers who want one of any pups these two dogs might produce in the future, and like Willie, we're on the road again. For the next four hours, I watch in a daze as flat grassland with spreading trees and steep, rugged mountains in the near distance flow past the car window. Just before the town of David, we stop again for gas. It's the same drill, except this time both Jack and I also have to use the bathroom and the dogs—now that the sun is up, cooking them under the glass of the hatchback—do drink a little water.

Once we turn off the Pan-American Highway and head up into the mountains, the scenery changes dramatically. The dogs are no longer in a glass oven. Steep mountains and dense trees block the sun, and as we wind our way higher and higher, the outside air becomes cooler. I'm beginning to wake up now. There are giant ferns everywhere and plants with leaves much bigger than an elephant's ear. A thousand shades of green cover steep mountain sides. The cab struggles up and down the other side of mountain after mountain until, at the peaks, we are riding in clouds, barely able to see the 1,000-foot drop on my side of the car or the jungle-covered mountain on the driver's side.

With the sharp turns, steep grade, and age of our vehicle, we're making slow progress through this country. Which is just great with me. No need to end the day by hurling down into whatever lies at the bottom of one of these green gorges. The dogs, however, are becoming restless, and Jack asks the driver to stop so we can get them out for a little leg stretching. There's no place to pull over here. It'll have to wait for a little town or a wide spot in the road. The taxi seems to be going slower and slower the higher we climb up these mountains, and—I know I worry about everything, but really—wasn't the car making an odd clacking noise earlier?

At a small crossroads, the taxi pulls over and stops. We get the dogs out and walk them along the road. Our driver, Manuel, hails a pick-up truck taxi and begins a conversation with the driver. Friends of his? No. It turns out our ride in his taxi is over. There are still several higher mountains between us and the tiny town of Almirante where we will take a boat to the islands, but the little hatchback isn't going to make it any further.

Jack, Manuel, and the new driver come to an agreement about how to divide up the money that we have already paid Manuel to get us to Almirante. We're on a mountain top with all our luggage and two dogs. I mean really, even Jack can't negotiate us cheaply out of this mess. But they eventually come to an agreement which only ends up costing us a couple hundred dollars more than it would have if the original taxi had made it the full distance he contracted with us to go.

Our dogs have never been taught to ride in the back of a pickup. Jack thinks we can tie their leads to the bumper, and they'll stay put. I'm not so sure. Especially if we go through a little town with chickens, goats, pigs, dogs, or—horror of horrors—cats. It turns out to be a moot point anyway, although the two of us manage to frustrate each other and raise our voices and blood pressures while we stand on the side of the road with our luggage piled at our feet and argue about it. There's no place to tie the leashes. No roll bar, no side grips. No bumper.

So, the luggage goes inside behind the seat in the cab, and all four of us—Jack, me, and both dogs—ride in the bed of the pickup. Here's a tip for you. If you ever ride in this delightful fashion, sit with your back to the cab. Yeah, I know. Duh! But it's been years since I rode in a pickup bed. Jack sits with his back resting against the cab. Chesty is at Jack's side, ears up and eyes round in the excitement of yet another experience. Or perhaps the dog's just excited that his legs still function, and he's not completely cooked after being crammed into the hatchback for ten hours. I face the front of the pickup and Rocca lies across my lap. With her weight holding me in place, there's no possibility I'm going to slide around on the slatted, wooden bed of the truck. Which is another thing. If you ever have to ride like this, try to find a pickup that doesn't have wooden slats over the metal floor. It's not as comfortable as you might think.

"Isn't this an adventure?" Jack grins as we pull away, waving goodbye to Manuel.

I try to grin bravely. I really do, but before I can get the expression fixed on my face, the driver pulls out. Within moments, I am nostalgic for the old hatchback oven. This driver, I don't know his name, let's call him Young Asshole, seems to think he is in a race. Which he may be. With death. Which is going to find all of us very soon if Young Asshole doesn't slow the fuck down!

Careening up and down the mountains, the wooden slats shift, and the tires screech out a protest at each turn. I am frozen in place. The wind up here is cold and when we come to the mountain peaks and enter the cloud forest, it freezes my face in a death mask of grinning fear. I don't know how close we are to flying off the mountain, our battered bodies plunging to our deaths, because I cannot move my head without my glasses being torn from my face. I cannot remove my glasses without turning loose of the side of pickup and having myself and Rocca thrown completely out of the vehicle. Besides, I can't hold on to them. I'm already gripping anything I can reach with both hands, my feet are wedged against whatever shifting edge I can find, and my sphincter muscles are vacuum-sealed to the wooden slats.

This part of our adventure goes on for a little over two hours, or possibly two lifetimes. Eventually, the pickup stops, and we find ourselves in one of the filthiest little towns I've ever seen. Rolling down a rutted dirt road, the pickup is surrounded by young boys in faded shorts and dirty tank tops. Before we come to a full stop, the bigger kids have reached over the side of the truck and removed our backpacks. As Young Asshole opens the door of the truck, more hands reach into the back seat and extract our suitcases.

These urchins wear huge smiles and chatter to us in a softened variation of English with the vowels slightly elongated, the ends of the words dropped a little, and the rhythm of the language shifted just to the left of center. I'm sure I'll come to love this Caribbean idiom at some point. But not now. Now I would like them to take their dirty little hands off my luggage and stop directing me to the dock and leave me the hell alone so I can get my legs to move once more and extradite myself and my dog from the pickup bed.

Of course, to them, we look like lunatics arriving in their territory. Our hair sticks out behind us as though blow dried by a maniac on amphetamines. Grins are frozen on our faces—the result of the freezing wind working like a mini centrifuge. Our legs and backs unbend excruciatingly slowly, making us appear to be as old as dirt, and on the end of leather leads, we have two dogs who are bigger than any of the raggedy children surrounding us.

Now Young Asshole decides he wants more money. He yells and postures and waves his arms and cusses in two languages. I leave him to Jack and Chesty and follow the kids who have stolen our luggage. They lead me down a short wooden pier and into a tin-roofed shed where local people sit on dilapidated wooden benches with plastic bags of supplies at their feet. The pier inside the shed is floating, and Rocca isn't thrilled with this new experience, but she comes right along beside me. People get up and move so she and I can have a bench all to ourselves. They avoid eye contact with me exactly as I do when I encounter a crazy person in a public place.

The children have stacked our luggage on the pier and now demand money for their labor. I give a dollar to a little guy in a red tank top that says, "Oregon State Beavers." This turns out to be a mistake. I have no idea which kid packed what, and now all of them have their hands out begging for money. Jack is still arguing with the driver. I begin to think I'd better forget the luggage and go backup my husband when Chesty barks. It's not a playful sound. Rocca, hearing Chesty, leaps to her feet and produces one of her roaring growls. The kids around me scatter, and I hear Jack walking along the pier and the taxi driving away.

We wait side by side on our bench, the dogs at each end, slowly rising and falling with the movement of the pier. The luggage is all there, stacked haphazardly among fish guts and candy wrappers and plastic bottles of water. I begin to get the feeling back in my right butt cheek. That's good news. I'm sure the left cheek will return to life soon.

Neither of us say a word to each other. Though Jack flirts with a little girl about a year old who's cuddled in her mama's arms across the pier from us. He makes a popping noise, putting his index finger in the side of his mouth and pulling it out quickly. Or something. I don't actually know how in the hell he makes the noise. It's loud and entertains the child at the same time it irritates the crap out of me.

We watch a small wooden panga boat make its way across the water to us. One person at the motor and two others bailing. They're not removing water especially urgently, but they are emptying modified plastic water jugs over the side of the boat at a regular rate. The people on the dock begin to shift and gather their possessions.

Huh. You don't suppose this is our boat to the islands?

"Here it is," Jack says, as though this is a good thing.

There's really nothing else to do but get on the boat. We sure as hell can't go back the way we just came. Our luggage is distributed in the swishing water at the bottom of the panga. I look at the space between its side and the floating dock. If my dog falls leaping into this boat, she's going to be smashed between the two and how in the hell am I going to lift her out? It's like riding a bicycle and staring so hard at the rock you want to avoid that you steer right for it. It's best to look down the road a bit and just keep pedaling.

Jack steps across the watery divide, and Chesty leaps in his usual rambunctious fashion. Unfortunately, this is Chesty's first time getting on a boat, and he's not prepared for either the slickness of an old wood boat or the way it moves when he lands. He slides sideways, recovers himself at the feet of a Kuna Indian family who watch stoically as though wondering how many appendages they'll have on their arrival at home today. Slipping and sliding on the wet, curved bottom of the boat, Chesty's tail is going in ever faster circles, eyes are round and sparkling.

"Gosh Dad, this is even more fun than the ride in the back of the pickup."

Rocca watches all this from my side on the pier. When I step across and onto the boat, she won't budge. She hunkers down and gives me her best mule impersonation—front feet straight out, body leaning back against the tug of the leash. I know from experience that you can't make a 148-pound dog do anything she doesn't want to do. I coax and entice and beg. Nope. She's not leaving the pier. Everyone on the boat is now involved in this drama. Some of them appear to look around for the candid camera.

"Just tell her to come," Jack instructs me.

"I'm afraid she's going to end up between the boat and the pier!"

"Well, if you keep worrying about it, she probably is," he says. "Take Chesty. Give her to me."

I'm emotionally torn as I watch him with Rocca. I really don't want him to be right. But I don't want my dog to fall either.

Jack tugs Rocca's lead and tells her to load in his best top-dog voice.

Rocca sits, her body leaning back against the leash and her front legs stiff as she braces herself backward. Exactly like that mule Yosemite Sam always had such a hard time motivating. The two bailers now come to the rescue. They get up on the pier and pull the boat tight against it, leaving no looming space between. Now all Rocca has to do is go from one moving object to another.

She lies down and inches her way forward. The two helpers grin and coax, Jack encourages. It takes her a full five minutes, but she manages to get on the boat, where she immediately slips sideways and lands on her side in the mucky water at the bottom. As she rights herself, she looks up at Jack and gives him a look that very clearly expresses her opinion of this little part of the adventure. She makes a sound somewhere between a moan and a growl and makes her way to me where she continues to glare at Jack.

I'm sure I don't know where she learned such an attitude.

Salt water in my face, a fresh ocean breeze in my stiff hair, I'm a happy woman. For the moment. And I'm taking this moment. It's pleasant. Nothing is required of me but to sit and watch the two young men bail water while I enjoy the ride. The scenery is glorious. Jungle green right down to the shoreline on the mainland, as well as on the small islands off to our right. I see this all through a misty haze as my glasses are speckled with sea spray from my spot at the far right side at the back of the boat. Still, we don't appear to be in danger of sinking, and this is a lot more pleasant than the pickup ride over the mountains.

Now that she's made it onto the boat, Rocca sits quietly at my side—her giant head, protected by the sides of the boat, rests under my hand. Chesty sits next to Jack on the bench seat of the boat. His tongue lolls from the side of his face as the wind blows salt spray over him. He looks around at everything, seemingly having himself a gay ol' time. That's our boy.

An hour or so later, we draw up at the island of Colón on Bocas del Toro. The small floating dock where we tie up is marginally cleaner than the one at Almirante. Or maybe I'm just getting used to the filth. Our fellow passengers disembark, and we maneuver our old bodies and dogs off the boat and onto the pier. Again, Chesty jumps mindlessly onto the dock while Rocca works her way across in her low crawl. Our luggage is gathered from the bottom of the boat and tossed up onto the dock. Jack goes to find us a taxi. I stay with the luggage. We have two medium-sized suitcases and two daypacks. As the second soggy suitcase hits the dock, it breaks open, spilling clothes and papers along the pier and into the water.

I gather up the clothes. The papers sink in the water between the boat and the dock, already gone to rest on the muddy bottom below. I have no idea what papers they might be. Tax information? Thirty years' worth of my writing? Whatever they are, they're gone now. I scramble along the dock, scoop up underwear and shampoo, stuff everything back into the suitcase in a wet, wadded mess. The luggage lid is sprung and won't close completely so I hold it shut and look around for a rope or something with which to tie it. Jack and Chesty stride back down the incline of the pier.

"What are you waiting for? Come on. I got us a taxi. Another pickup," he informs me as though this is a big accomplishment.

"The suitcase fell open. A bunch of stuff fell in the water. I can't get the lid to close." I'm reduced now to the short, stumpy sentences of the very young or the mentally ill.

That's what I say, but this is what Jack hears:

"Blah blah blah, whine, moan, and piss."

He picks up the other suitcase and both backpacks, heads up the ramp, leaving me to hug the ruptured suitcase against my chest and struggle with Rocca. Chesty and Jack have already arranged themselves in the truck when Rocca and I get there and heave our aching bodies up into the metal bed. This time, I am smart enough to sit with my back to the cab of the truck. As it turns out, it doesn't matter because we're only going a few slow blocks over bumpy sand roads to get to our hotel. The one where we have reservations for us and *the dogs*.

We pull up to the Hotelito del Mar and drag ourselves, our soggy, broken luggage, and our dogs onto the sand. The woman who manages this small hotel is a large, friendly, black woman. Until she sees the dogs. Then she transforms into a screaming, raving, wild woman, waves her hands in the air, and backs away screaming, "No! No! No!"

We attempt to explain about the reservations and how we spoke with someone here, at this hotel, who understood about the dogs. All we get is more screeching, more variations of the dance of terror and some additional, "No! No! No!"

The woman locks herself in the hotel's tiny office, peers at us from the window. We can still hear "No!" from out here in the sun, on the sand, where we stand with all our earthly possessions. The taxi driver recovers more quickly than do we. He loads our luggage back in the truck and motions for us to climb back in. Since we can't think of anything else to do, we follow his directions.

Thus begins our first tour of Bocas. Old, wooden plantation houses and little cement shacks with tin roofs are piled higgledy-piggledy on each other. Garbage is scattered everywhere. A small park has huge piles of trash raked up under each spreading tree and beside each bench. The roads are sand interspersed with mud puddles. But my most powerful first impression of Bocas is of the hundreds of black buzzards that roost on the roofs and in the palm trees. A group of these dull-black birds strut along a wooden sidewalk behind a gathering of little boys who wear nothing but swimming trunks, the buzzards like pet dogs escorting their charges on a walk.

Our taxi driver tries four hotels. We know the drill by now. I wait in the truck with both dogs where I attempt to keep Chesty from going bonkers trying to chase the buzzards, while Jack tries to get us a room. He doesn't talk sweet enough, and even the old American trick of waving money around doesn't help, so we move on. Finally we find the Casitas del Mar, a small American-run hotel. The owner/manager, Sally, takes one look at the dogs and says, not "no," but "no fucking way."

By this time, I'm drinking my own urine and waiting for my trapped arm to rot. An odd phenomenon has started where my head begins to shake, and then the movement continues on down my body until I'm having a sort of mini-seizure. Perhaps I have sun stroke. Sally doesn't want the dogs in her hotel, but neither does she want a *gringa* having a nervous breakdown on her patio. She lets us have a room. I don't even say thank you. I walk to the room in a trancelike state, sit on the edge of the bed, and wait for the feeling to come back into my butt and legs and the shaking to stop.

"There," says Jack as he comes inside after making all the arrangements with Sally, "I told you there wouldn't be any problem getting a room with the dogs."

I don't kill him with my bare hands.

THIRTEEN
THE PRICE SMART IS WHERE?

THERE OUGHT TO be an awards show for marriage. A Golden Globe or Oscar or, at the very least, a sort of Nobel Prize for the Institute of Holy Matrimony. I want recognition, Goddamnit! The nominees this year are:

Paula Smith, for surviving the first year of raising twins while her Lance Corporal husband served as a Marine in Afghanistan.

Cynthia Watson, for putting her husband, John, through law school and then finding herself pregnant before she could begin her own college degree.

And Pamela Foster, for relocating to the Republic of Panama with her husband and two elephant-sized dogs, and once she realized she was stuck there with no way to return and no way to get her husband to listen to her, did not follow through on any of the dozen ways she dreamed up to kill him dead.

And the winner is...

I could stand and hug my husband dramatically before winding my way through the glamorous crowd, up the steps to the stage to clutch my award to my heaving breasts. I can picture the trophy too. A gold-plated jackass, his hind feet kicking against the air, or maybe a tiny monkey, an asinine smile on its face and its hands over its head as though swinging from some imaginary support.

I know what I'd say in my acceptance speech.

"I'd like to thank the Academy. All the people who helped me along the way. As for my husband, Jack, I'd like to say that if, when I get back to my seat, he leans over to me and says, 'See Honey, I told you it would all work out okay,' I'm going to bludgeon him to death on national television with my golden jackass."

———————

I N BOCAS, WE spend our first night on the long sought-after islands in a small hotel room, training the dogs not to bark at drunks leaning against our door, firecrackers that split the night in staccato imitations of machine gun fire, or the high notes hit by the Caribbean musicians crooning Bob Marley tunes across the street. This is one of those nights when time sticks, traps me in a swirling cauldron of fear, despair, and anger. There ought to be hope as well. We're here. We did make it to the islands.

But, my God, this island? This is not my idea of paradise. It's filthy— and by the way, where the fuck is the Price Smart? Didn't all those blogs and chat rooms on the internet talk about a Price Smart twenty minutes from Bocas Town? I haven't seen even a supermarket, just a few Latin American-style *fondas* or *tiendas*. Small local markets where I know from experience the chocolate bars are going to be speckled white from having melted a dozen times before purchase, and the meat counter is going to smell like, well, like raw, warm meat. It's also expensive here. Los Angeles prices and third world conditions. What the hell?

We walked the dogs along the main street before we gave up and came to bed. We checked out restaurant menus as we walked. The only inexpensive food comes from little hole-in-the-wall cafeteria style cafés where everyone eats bunkhouse style, or as I like to call it, all wadded up together. The main dishes seemed to be tough meat marinated in tomato sauce with sides of fried plantains and greasy fried rice. Jack loves this kind of food and atmosphere. I'm less thrilled.

Lying awake, the light from the bar across the street making a pale flashing streak of yellow across the bed from between the drawn curtains, Rocca and I are serenaded by the snores of Jack and Chesty. It's a lullaby with which we're familiar. I have one hand dangling off the side and resting on Rocca's head so I can quickly correct her tendency to bark in protection from the noises outside the room. She's not going to fall asleep until I do.

Jack startles in his sleep each time a line of firecrackers splits the night, which causes Chesty to leap up and bark. I can only control one dog at a time. I should enjoy tonight's sleep in a real bed as by this time tomorrow, after a night of barking and disturbing the other hotel guests, I imagine we'll be sleeping on the street. Maybe curled up under one of the wooden sidewalks with the hermit crabs and black vultures.

Things quiet down outside just before dawn, and I must have fallen asleep because when Jack wakes me the next morning with a cup of coffee in a paper cup, I'm dreaming that I'm caught in a whirlpool, swallowing dirty, turbulent water and not even fighting that hard to escape.

"Morning, love. I brought you coffee." He smiles at me.

Is there anything more irritating than the person you're trying to be angry with acting all sweet and nice? I drag myself up in bed to accept the offering of caffeine. This ain't our first rodeo. One of the things Jack and I have learned over the years is that even when you'd like to gut your spouse while wearing a big, saliva-dripping grin, it's important to be polite and considerate to each other. Whatever situation we're in at the moment—and we've been in some beauties—will pass, and we'll still be together and we'll still love one another. This is the theory anyway. It's difficult to believe, however, when you're drinking your own urine. And speaking of drinking piss, where the hell did he find this dark liquid that is being passed off as coffee?

I'd like to pull the covers over my head and go back to sleep, but we need to walk the dogs, and Jack is looking forward to another lovely dining experience in yet another grease-coated restaurant he's found off an alley near the hotel. So I get up, pull on my clothes, and get myself as ready for the day as I can manage. My shaking is back, but it's limited to the right side of my body, so I'm adjusting pretty well to our new situation.

The side of Bocas Town that frames the Caribbean is covered with hotels and restaurants. Each has a floating dock that extends out over the blue sea where customers sit and gaze across at the emerald islands that dot the coast and watch the folks coming across the water in their *pangas* and canoes to pick up supplies from the big city of Bocas Town. These touristy docks are scenic and inviting and very expensive.

The main street is packed and sand lined with wooden sidewalks and plantation-style teak buildings painted various shades of pastel long ago, during the heyday of exploitation by The United Fruit Company. The entire main street is two blocks long. From here, the town meanders along the edge of the island with dilapidated cement and wooden shacks sitting side by side with well-maintained, brightly-painted, two-story houses. Dogs, dying of mange and neglect, wander the sandy streets, trailed by the ever-present, leathery, black buzzards biding their time.

On Main Street, the people are mostly *gringos*. Rich *gringos* with casual Land's End shorts, crocodile logo shirts, and $100 haircuts, mixed with leather-skinned *gringos* who appear to have been rode hard and put up wet. After Jack's breakfast, he appeases me by agreeing to coffee at one of the little waterside cafés. Here we discover that the rich *gringos* are mostly real estate salespeople, and the ones that look as though they've fallen into a nightmare of dashed dreams and never-ending work are the former's victims.

We sit and watch the boats pull in from the outer islands. I do not see a single *gringo* manning these boats who smiles. Not one time. The islands in the distance look spectacular. Lush green edged by a narrow strip of pure white set in deep blue ocean. None of these islands can be more than a foot or two above sea level at their highest point, and they are tiny, for the most part, just a few acres in size. They're beautiful, but can they possibly be habitable?

Sitting and sipping our delicious cappuccinos, the dogs attract the attention of the real estate folks on their morning round-up. Here's what we learn our first morning in town:

English is spoken with a charming Caribbean lilt, but only in tiny pockets on the Atlantic edge of the country. Throughout the remainder of the land, various Spanish dialects reign. If you want to get anything done in this country, you must speak Spanish or hire someone who does.

Foreigners cannot actually own land here in Bocas. They rent for ninety-nine years from the government of Panama. This is being changed, and foreigners will be grandfathered in and handed a clear title to their land within the next year. That's why the land here is such a bargain right now. If we wait to buy, even for a few months, the whole ball of wax could shift, and the prices will double or triple. In some cases, people will be getting ten times or more what they paid for their land.

Ah... yeah.

Gringos discovered these islands about five years ago. A number of them came in and bought up huge tracts of land and whole islands from the locals who have lived here in peace for all the years before the arrival of these realtors. These white salespeople have been heavily marketing the area ever since they received their muddy rights to the land. This we learned—surprise, surprise, not from a real estate agent—from an old guy sitting at a corner table who climbed out of a small, wooden panga just after we sat down.

Panama does not license its real estate agents. Therefore, everyone in the country is selling property. The standard deal is, if a person, any person, brings together a buyer and a seller, that facilitator gets five percent of the purchase price of the property. This explains why every waiter, bartender, and taxi driver knows someone who has property to sell you.

Real estate fraud is the number one pastime in Panama. I'm pretty sure that setting off firecrackers is the not-too-distant second, super-fun entertainment. The mayor of Bocas is in jail for land fraud. He sold a sizable portion of the islands to *gringos*. Evidently, this land wasn't owned by him, and he didn't notify the people who did own it.

The land prices that we saw on the internet before we came down are no longer valid because property values are doubling and tripling each and every month or when a new batch of suckers arrives on the banana boat. Those small pieces of beautiful islands for which we came all this way are not titled and cost more than we'll ever have to spend.

It's true there is a Price Smart twenty minutes from Bocas Town. Twenty minutes by plane to the city of David and then a short taxi ride to the store.

By the time we've finished our cappuccinos and first fact-finding tour, the shaking has extended to the left side of my body, but hey, we're here, and there must be some way to make this dream work. Other people are doing it. The place is chockablock with *gringos*. *Gringos* that resemble chain gang prisoners from hell, but still, it cannot be a mistake for us to have come all this way. That would mean we were wrong to come. Surely not. There must be some other explanation.

With the dogs, we explore the town a little more in hope of finding some hidden garden spot. But no, it's all pretty much the same. A few nice houses, every one of which is crammed up against little shacks surrounded by garbage and dirt. The air smells of fresh ocean breeze, burning plastic, and rotting garbage. On the plus side, the reason for the giant stacks of trash in the park was the Independence Day celebration the day before we got here. The garbage men are busy this morning hauling stinky piles away as fast as they can in broken-down, rusting wheelbarrows. I decide not to think about where, exactly, on an island, they're dumping all this garbage.

Back at the hotel room, I try to think over the noise of the eternal blaring loop in my head, the constant refrain of "Stupid! Stupid! Stupid! Why did I sell the house in Arizona? What was I thinking to come here?"

"I wanna go home," I whine to Jack, knowing that we have no home. We sold our home. Oh God! We're homeless.

"We just got here. We don't even know what's here yet."

"I haven't seen anyplace where I want to live on this island!" I wail and cry.

"We knew we didn't want to live here in town. We're looking to find a place on one of the smaller islands, remember?"

"The people coming from those islands don't look happy."

"Well, of course not. They're running errands when they're here. On their peaceful islands, I'm sure they're happy and enjoying life."

"I'm going back to bed."

"I'm going out to find us a place to rent so we have some place to live while we locate exactly the right property for us."

I pull the covers over my head, Rocca collapses on the floor under my hand, and Jack and Chesty shut the door none too gently behind them. I'm not usually like this. Really. I'm normally adventurous and provide good backup for Jack. I may be able to do that here too if I can just stop these crying jags and the uncontrollable shaking.

FOURTEEN
GOD SPEAKS THROUGH HUGH GRANT

LYING IN BED tonight, our second night in Bocas, Rocca on the floor beside the bed, my hand on her big head, I do my best to relax. My best isn't doing the trick. The shaking has been reduced to an occasional head twitch. I could maybe fall asleep in between the jerks and starts, except that I now have frog legs. The medical name for this is Restless Leg Syndrome. Frog legs is a much more descriptive term. Just as I start to relax, my legs leap, bullfrog style, as though trying desperately to lift me out of an algae-filled pond where hungry snakes and possibly even alligators lurk.

I attempt to lie still and imagine myself in a sanctuary of some kind and then begin my descent down a mental staircase into a deeper and still deeper peace. Well, first of all, it's hard to lie still when the bottom half of you thinks it's a leaping frog and the top half is in a state I can only describe as Shake, Twitch, and Roll. Still, this is all I know to do, so I try to take myself mentally to a safe place. Except, where exactly would that be?

It's not here in this hotel room with firecrackers and drunks reigning right outside the door. It's not back in my bed in Arizona. Someone else is sleeping in that bed. Maybe a quiet place of dense, lush green in the redwood forest back in my childhood home of Humboldt County, California? No, that wouldn't really be safe either. Anyone might bebop down the forest trail and discover me there, sitting cross-legged among the ferns and pretending to be safe. And another thing, where would my dogs be while I was meditating in the green forest of home? Are they in a safe place? All right, that image isn't working. I try to imagine that we find a lovely, peaceful little house here on Bocas with green jungle all around and the blue sea at our doorstep.

Nope, my imagination isn't that good.

Okay. Maybe I'm taking this safety thing too literally. I mean, really. Absolute safety is an illusion. We're never safe. Not for one single second of our whole entire lives. Pain, destruction, and death can come through any door at any time. Gee, this line of thinking isn't doing much to help me relax and get to sleep.

The young English couple in the room next to ours is home from their evening out. They fumble with the key to their room. Rocca does her low growl, but she does not bark. Good girl. Chesty, like Jack, sleeps through the whole thing.

Have I mentioned that the dogs are sleeping in their collars with their leashes attached, the loop end of the leather in our hands? There's a low window in this tiny room, lovely for looking out at the sandy street that fronts the hotel, not good for the dogs who have learned that they can stand flat-footed in the room and see anything outside that needs killing. Of course, we have the drapes drawn, which means the dogs simply push them aside, the material draped over their heads like burkas, and peek through the glass. Not good for the drapes or for anyone walking by who will most likely need to find a laundry service when a deafening bark erupts from two massive dogs behind a thin window of glass mere inches away.

The dogs are used to getting a bath every Saturday, and they haven't had one since we left Arizona. So far, we haven't found a room with a detachable shower head, and it's impossible to rinse them properly without one. Maybe tomorrow we'll see if Sally will let us use the hose out back to give them a good scrub. They both smell a bit like the rotten, fishy water from the bottom of the boat on which we arrived in this paradise. Okay, good plan, but this isn't helping me to fall asleep either.

Forget the hunt for a safe place, I'll try the old standby. Prayer. *Be still and know that I am God.* That's a good place to start. Here we go, bullfrog legs and all, this might actually be my safe place. No begging for help, no thanking the supreme power for gifts he's given, just relax in the knowledge of God. Shush now. No thinking. Be quiet. Listen for the whispering voice of God.

"POSITIVELY BRILLIANT PLAN, LUV. BOCAS DEL TORO. THE PLACE IS A SHITHOLE, AND THE BEERS ARE FIVE DOLLARS A POP."

God sounds like Hugh Grant? And complains about the price of beer?

Ah, the British couple next door. The two bathrooms share a vent which brings their Cockney accents into bed with us. Still, just because the voice came through the vocal cords of a young, beer-drinking Brit doesn't mean it wasn't God speaking.

Well okay, maybe it does, but still, it makes me wonder.

The last time I look at the bedside clock, it's blinking a luminous green 3:22. The next time I look, it's flashing 6:57, and I smell coffee. Must be time to rise and shine and see what fresh hell today brings.

"Morning, Love, relax and drink your coffee. Chesty and I have already been for our walk. I'll take Rocca with me here in a minute and try again to find us a house to rent."

My eyes are still glued shut, and my brain isn't processing words yet, so I just nod my head and cradle my paper cup of coffee.

By the time I can see the bottom of the cup, I'm awake enough to ask, "Are you sure we should be looking for a place to rent? Maybe we'd be better off cutting our losses and figuring out where we want to go from here."

"We've been over this. We just got here. We don't know anything about the place yet. We'll rent a house for a few months and take our time and find the perfect spot. You'll see. It'll all work out."

Will we find this as-yet-undiscovered haven before I come completely and irreversibly undone? I don't ask this nagging question. Instead, I stare silently into the bottom of my empty paper cup and try not to twitch.

"Rocca and I will bring you another cup of coffee before we head up the road to find those realtors I talked to yesterday. They are supposed to have houses lined up for me to see today."

I nod, Jack gives me Chesty's lead, he takes Rocca's, and away he goes. My husband is a force of nature. Once he gets rolling, the momentum will carry him along for quite a long way. Which is good, because my forward moving days have ended for the moment. Even Jack is only going to be able to carry along two dogs and a dead-to-the-world wife for so long. I seriously need to snap out of this obsessive anxiety and get on with the adventure, so I can pull my own weight.

Deep in my own funk, I don't notice that Chesty has homed in on prey until he leaps across the bed and launches himself at the wall above the headboard, hot on the trail of a resident gecko. Unfortunately, I am still in the bed that he's using as a launch pad. By the time I get him down from the wall and off the bed, Jack and Rocca have returned with my second cup of coffee, and that damn shaking has come back to claim my head and right arm. We will, I'm convinced, be thrown out of this hotel by tonight when Sally attempts to reclaim her room before our unruly dogs completely destroy it.

"Chesty saw a gecko," I tell Jack as I reach through the door to take the steaming cup.

"Ha, ha, ha," says Jack. "That's my boy. I'll see you in a while."

And he's gone—before I can explain about the scratch marks on my legs and stomach or my certainty that we'll be needing another place to stay by tonight. Probably just as well.

By the time I've had my second cup of coffee, Chesty is asleep. I'd like to take a shower. I guess I can shut Chesty in the bathroom with me. The room's not that big, but the dog's good at fitting himself into tight spaces. No way in hell I can leave him out here with the attack geckos. I wake up my dog and into the bathroom we go. Chesty is wearing what I call his "round-eyed look"—the demeanor that signifies he's feeling playful. I don't especially want a rambunctious, giant dog with me while I'm naked in a tiny space, but not knowing any other way to get my shower, I go ahead with the plan.

The water isn't hot. It isn't even warm. Well. This is going to be a fast shower, and maybe I'll forget about washing my hair. When that first blast of cold water hits me, I squeal. Chesty leaps into the shower with me. His front half fits. His back half is still dry. He looks around, tries to discover from what I need rescuing when, low and behold, he spots another damn attack gecko. His eyes sparkle like a demon. He uses the closest support he can find to reach the threat. Which is me. Naked. Wet. Me. The gecko, thank you God for small favors, disappears into a crack in the plaster, and I manage to get Chesty out of the shower while sustaining only a couple of major abrasions.

Toweling off, examining the damage, I tell my boy, "Thank you so much, Chesty, for rescuing me from the terribly dangerous, three-inch lizard, but next time, perhaps you could do so without ripping off half my skin."

He looks up at me, his eyes still round, his tail wagging in circles. *"You're welcome Mom. Just call me The Great Lizard Chaser!"*

When I'm dry, I use the same towel to rub off as much of the water as I can from Chesty's front half. He thinks this a great game called "Grab the Towel and Pull." I manage to get the towel away from him with only one or two tooth marks in the cotton. Maybe we can just offer to buy all the bedding and towels in the room before we leave. We've got to get out of here soon. Between gecko chasing, tug of war, and wiping their mouths along the sides of the bed every chance they get, this tiny little room is quickly becoming a dog kennel where two people also hang out.

Just as I finish dressing, the maid comes to the door to clean the room for the day. This will be where she discovers the damage the dogs have done, and we're thrown out on our ears to fend off the buzzards. Still, nothing to be done about it, so Chesty and I vacate the premises so she can clean and we can get some exercise. We walk around town, down a few side roads, and along the wooden sidewalks of Main Street. This place is growing on me. Once I get rid of my preconceived ideas of what I thought it would be, maybe it will turn out to be all right.

Chesty and I sit on a bench overlooking the dirt road and watch people stroll past or arrive from the other islands in various boats. The locals here are mostly Indians and Blacks. The Blacks are physically beautiful people. Tall and regal, the young are thin and long-boned, the older people wider and more imposing. I don't know from what part of Africa their ancestors were ripped, but these are fine-looking folk. Think Michael Jordan and Queen Latifa, if Michael and the Queen were poor and lived in a place where growing bananas and fishing had been the way of life for twenty generations or so.

Now, these same beautiful people have discovered they can make more money catering to tourists than they can working for United Fruit or pulling fish from the sea. The young men roam the sidewalks and offer to take tourists fishing or snorkeling or sightseeing on the other islands. The women work as waitresses in expensive restaurants or maids in the hotels. They all have family land they'd like to sell, very cheap—a bargain for us, their brand-new, special friend.

Coming down the sidewalk from the den of realtor's offices, stomps Jack. He's no longer whistling, though as he gets near, I can hear him singing to himself that old Animals hit, "We gotta get outta this place, if it's the last thing we ever do."

Probably not a good omen.

"Hey, any luck finding a place to rent?" I greet him.

"These assholes," he says. "They showed me five places. Three of them were dumps. I mean *shacks*. One didn't even have running water and they wanted six hundred dollars a month! The other two were all right, but they want twelve hundred dollars a month for them."

"Well, maybe that's just how much rent is here. If we want to stay until we find a place to buy, we just have to pay it."

"Let's have lunch," he growls. "And I'm not paying these assholes three times what a house is worth. We'll find someplace. But not through one of these realtors."

Occasionally, I know when to shut up. This isn't one of those times.

"But Jack, we need to get the dogs out of that little hotel room and into someplace with a fenced yard. Did any of these places have fenced yards?"

"I'll find us a place, don't worry about it. I'll ask around, and we'll find one with a yard. One that we can afford."

His growl has reached that depth that clearly says, "end of discussion." I let it go. For now. But this isn't over. I don't understand why we can't rent one of the over-priced places for just a month and then look for something else priced more reasonably. All I really care about right now is getting the dogs and us into someplace where we'll all be safe. Well, relatively safe, safer than a tiny hotel room that sits right on a busy tourist town street.

Over lunch, which is at one of the greasy spoons on the wrong side of Main Street, I say, just to make conversation, "Maybe we can give the dogs a bath this afternoon. There's a hose out back of the hotel. Sally probably wouldn't mind."

Jack stares off into space. Maybe he heard me. Maybe he didn't.

A little later, I try, "Did something happen to piss you off? Did you have a fight with one of the realtors or something?"

He gives one of his "I can't explain it to a woman as stupid as you are" sighs and says, "Nothing happened. These guys are just rip-off artists, and it pisses me off."

Okay. So now what do we do? I think about mentioning to him that the voice of God spoke to me last night and told me to get the fuck out of this shithole, but this seems unlikely to have a positive effect on his mood. I eat my greasy meat and squeeze my fingernails into my palms in order to distract myself from Chesty's leash, lying loose in Jack's lap while my husband uses both hands to cut and eat his food. Not a good time to point out that he doesn't have his dog under control. The gods owe me one. I pull in this marker and ask for no stray cat, or dog, or wandering buzzard, or stalking gecko to wander by and attract the attention of our great, furry protector while Jack finishes his meal.

FIFTEEN
THE QUAGMIRE THICKENS AND ROCCA ATTRACTS A FOLLOWING

I T'S THE SMALL things that seem to bother me the most. The little comforts of daily life that are lacking, which seem to carry an inappropriate psychic weight. I want to click my heels together three times and transport myself back to my abandoned life, just long enough to sit in my comfortable chair and drink a cup of coffee from my favorite mug. While I'm there, maybe I'll walk around the yard and enjoy my flowers, deadhead a few roses and refill the hummingbird feeders. Not the kind of momentous experiences that entice me to stay forever in one place, but that are nevertheless sorely missed when they're gone.

Now that we're here, on the fabled Bocas del Toro islands, Jack's PTSD has seized him by the throat. First of all, he has a number of what he calls "Combat Anniversary Dates" in November. His body and muscles remember these traumatic events even as his mind attempts to shut them out. That old western philosophical concept of the separation of mind and body doesn't hold up under reality.

But, Jack and I, we're used to these November and December doldrums. This year, we've added to his anniversary dates the additional stress of being responsible for an addled and possibly mentally-ill wife and two increasingly tense dogs, in a situation that is turning out one hell of lot different than he envisioned when we left Arizona. He knows we can't stay in this hotel for much longer without the dogs and me coming unglued.

The center is no longer holding. But he hasn't been successful in finding us anywhere else to go. While he's much less worried than I am about potential dangers, such as the dogs darting out the hotel room door or leaping free of a loosely held leash to chase a cat, he also knows that if something like that does happen I'm, first of all, going to blame him, and second, I'm probably not going to handle it well. I know he's got to be fed up to his eyeballs with my shaking and crying, my fears and obsessions.

So, he's tense. He stops singing and starts to mumble. The more I shake, the angrier he becomes, and the angrier he is, the more I shake, and the more... well, you get the idea. After working throughout our marriage to be a helpmate, I have become a dependent. I see clearly what's happening. I'm aware of the bones of the marriage disintegrating. I understand that soon, our only option is going to be the hacking off of an appendage or two. Yet I can't make it stop. Instead, I stare at those circling buzzards and try to build my courage enough to begin the amputation of my hopes and expectations, figure out how to admit defeat and go on from here, crippled but still alive.

We spend the next two days holed up in the air-conditioned hotel room out of the heat, taking long walks morning and evening to help the dogs release energy. Both dogs, following our lead, have sunk into lassitude. Rocca especially has to be forced to leave the room. Once outside, she walks with her head down and no spring to her step. Chesty has energy and interest, but he too has toned his excitement down a few notches from his normal rambunctious self.

Walking in the cool of the mornings and in the dusky evening, Bocas begins to grow on me a little more each day. Maybe we could live here and enjoy ourselves. The people are friendly. The ocean, dotted with those verdant, green islands ringed in white sand, is gorgeous. The ramshackle wooden houses that appear thrown down higgledy-piggledy by some angry giant, do have a certain laid-back charm. I just have to be selective in framing my view. Look past the rotting garbage and the moldy walls, beyond the smell of burning plastic that permeates the island from three o'clock each afternoon until the nightly rains. Focus my attention on the simple beauty in the faded pastel houses and the laughing, naked children in the sandy streets. I might be able to get used to living here. The question remains, is that what I want?

While we walk with the dogs, we look at every bulletin board and ask everyone with whom we can strike up a conversation, "Do you know of a place to rent or buy?" They all know of places to buy. All these recommended houses and islands cost more money than we can afford, or they're rented lots on which you build your own home behind guarded gates, or they're huge tracts of land on the interior of an island with no water or electricity or sewer or possibility of living like anything but old, exhausted hippies. It becomes increasingly clear that to live here in the style we had hoped for, we need ten times more money than we have and twenty times the energy and stamina.

We do find places for rent, but none of them are appropriate for us and the dogs, or they exceed our budget. The houses we can afford are effectively shacks in which I know I cannot live and keep my cheerful outlook. Well, okay, perhaps that ship has sailed. Still, I'm not going to live in a patched wooden hovel with a tin roof and pay some greedy bastard $600 a month for the privilege. Of course, I don't know what else to do either.

Sally, the manager of the hotel, is as motivated to get us out of there as we are to move, and on our eighth day on the island, she finds us a place to rent. It's in a section of Bocas Town called Little Saigon for reasons that are never explained to me. The house is surrounded with an eighteen-inch cement footer topped by a cyclone fence. That sounds dog-proof all right. It's a two-story with the kitchen and one room at ground level and the two bedrooms, a living room, and bathroom upstairs. A balcony skirts two sides of the upstairs, and a deep shaded porch is downstairs. We walk down and peek at the house through the secure fence and agree to take it. $600 a month—we pay *three months* in advance to get it.

We can move in three days from now when the owners come to the island from the mainland to meet us and collect the rent. Now, I should feel hopeful. Instead, I can't help feeling as though we're still looking forward to the light at the end of the train tunnel. In the meantime, we keep searching for a place to buy. We talk with the Century 21 realtor about buying a tiny island just across from Bocas Town. $200,000.

The property is a little less than two acres in size with an existing structure. Structure. When even a realtor doesn't call it a house, you gotta assume it's a patched-together shack. Water is a catchment system, meaning you put up a large, blue plastic tank, elevated to increase pressure, and collect some of the rainwater that blesses these islands. Most years there's no problem, and you receive plenty of rainfall all year to keep the tank topped off. Electricity is produced by a generator or will be once we buy one. Gas for this machine will need to be carried to the island in a boat—which, given we'd be transporting all our groceries as well as our drinking water, dog food, and anything else we would need by boat, wouldn't be any major problem, according to Jack who's getting excited about owning an island.

He meets with the realtor to arrange a time to see the place, though he explains to her, "I'm not ready to commit to Bocas yet. My wife has been crying nonstop since our arrival."

"Oh," the realtor tells him with a knowing nod, "that will pass. All white women cry for the first six months they're here."

Jack relates this to me as a form of encouragement. I take it differently than he intends.

We talk to other people and discover that a foreigner can't actually own an island in Panama. Or any property that is ten miles from a national border or that touches the sea. Huh. We speak with the Century 21 realtor again.

"Yes, that's right," she tells us casually. "This island does not have a clear title. It's what's known as Right of Possession."

As far as we can ascertain, Rights of Possession are squatter's rights, and now this particular squatter is attempting to sell the island to some idiot with more money than brains. But I paraphrase. Legally, the island is still owned by the government of Panama, but that's no problem as the legislature is, even as we speak, changing the law so that everyone with a current Right of Possession will be given a coveted Clear Title. That's why this island is such a steal. The instant the law changes, this beautiful spot in the Caribbean is going to be worth, minimum, half a million.

Ah... yeah. Or, it seems to me, pessimistic skeptic that I am, that the government is going to decide to take all its land back from the whole mess of money-grubbing *gringos*, and the island is going to be worth less than zero dollars as the owner is expected to return the land to the condition it was in before he attempted to steal it from the country of Panama and its people.

Admitting a mistake must be just about the most difficult thing in the world to do. Certainly, I struggle with the concept. I will do almost anything to avoid looking reality in the face and saying simply, I messed up. I was wrong. I have created, all on my own, with no help from anyone else, a terrible situation and have no idea how to get myself out of this quagmire. I will even seriously consider living on a two-acre island or in a house surrounded by chicken pens and garbage. I will paint over a reality of hardship and stupidity, create an image of independence and adventure. I hate to be wrong.

Add to that the fact that, after everything we went through to get the dogs to these islands, I'm not sure I can handle getting them back off Bocas, and we have a recipe for depression, desperation, and really dumb decisions.

We continue to look at places for sale, hope against known reality that we will discover we've misjudged the islands. Pray it will turn out that Bocas del Toro really is an inexpensive paradise on earth.

A young woman realtor wearing short shorts and a halter top takes us by boat to see a nearly completed house on Bastimentos Island, the next island over. We join her under her home office at a rickety dock. Since both Jack and I need to have a look at the place, we have both dogs with us. No way we can leave them in the hotel room alone. Jesus God, what if Chesty saw another attack gecko, or Rocca decided to chew up a pillow in retaliation for abandonment? So, here we are again coaxing two dogs from a floating dock onto a bobbing boat.

It's raining. Of course. Bocas has two seasons—wet and wetter. We've arrived during the wetter season. Clever us. Chesty, true to form, leaps into the boat the instant Jack steps across and calls him. Unfortunately, in his exuberance, he slips on the wet aluminum, slides sideways, and slams into one of the metal seats that span the bottom of the boat. It looks like he's killed himself, or at the very least, broken a couple of ribs.

But he immediately jumps up, throws his head from side to side with his tongue lolling, and gives Jack a look that seems to say, *"I meant to do that. Didn't hurt me a bit. Now, where are we goin'? What'll we see? Can I sit next to you on the seat? Will there be cats to chase?"*

Rocca, unimpressed with her guy's antics, does her practiced slow crawl from pier to boat. Having successfully gotten into the boat with no mishaps, we take off across the channel to Bastimentos Island. There our sexy, young saleswoman pulls into a dock where two very tall, very beautiful, young black men wearing shorts, tank tops, and red-and-green crocheted hats tie up the boat and help the women disembark. They're not interested in assisting Jack, and the dogs they try to avoid altogether.

"*Perros bravos!*" they say when they see the dogs.

To which we reply enthusiastically, *"Si, claro. Muy bravo!"*, thinking this means "brave dog" when in fact, a more accurate translation is "trained attack dogs who are hoping to tear your balls off and eat them as tiny little snacks."

Now we follow Realtor Short Shorts along a muddy, garbage-strewn, dirt path past houses built of driftwood and scrap tin, naked black children, mangy dogs, ten thousand chickens, and two roosters. I'm pretty sure Jack sees none of this as he's directly behind a much better view. The house turns out to be a two-story cement building painted white. The exterior is completed, but the interior needs a little work. The kitchen and bathroom fixtures are about half done. The lot is just big enough so that we can squeeze past the outside walls on two sides. The front and back boundaries give enough room that we can all walk side by side. If we don't mind rubbing shoulders and hips together. Which Jack doesn't.

It's the shape of the lot that fascinates me. It looks as though someone has gotten a rabid monkey drunk, tied a string of firecrackers to his tail, turned him loose, and wherever the sparks flew, that's where they marked the property line. Zigzagged doesn't even begin to describe it. The house sits on a rocky beach. There's about twenty feet of actual ocean front, and the house is less than thirty feet from the flat, rocky shoreline. No other houses sit this close to the water on this little point. Which makes me wonder why that is, since all around the back of the house there is the usual collection of ramshackle dwellings thrown down by that aforementioned crazed giant.

Along the shoreline of this tiny finger jutting out into the sea is a garbage dump. Doesn't that make you wonder if the waves don't come in and remove this garbage periodically, prompting the local folks to deposit their trash here for nature's removal?

"Why is the house for sale when it's not completed?" Jack asks.

"The owners paid a contractor to build it, and the guy absconded with the money. They've come down three or four times a year for three years and worked on it each time, but the whole thing was really the husband's idea, and now that the wife has become hospitalized, they're forced to sell the place."

Wanna bet the wife isn't hospitalized so much as institutionalized? I'm thinking mental hospital or lock-up for the criminally insane because she tried to kill her husband for bringing her to this dump in the first place. Unfortunately for me, I can't blame my husband for our being here. It was my brilliant idea, remember? Of course, he shouldn't have encouraged me. In retrospect, locking me up until I came to my senses might have been a better response.

"How much are they asking again?" Jack asks as I, just to see if we'll get dizzy, walk the property line with Rocca.

"They're asking two hundred forty-five thousand cash, but I know they'll take less."

No shit. Before the next big storm washes it away with the garbage.

We return to the boat and find that a pack of neighborhood dogs have organized themselves into a skinny gang and appear to be waiting for Rocca and Chesty to pass back by. Chesty wiggles so hard he's in danger of throwing himself off the narrow path, down the embankment, and onto the rocks below. Rocca, with just about as much patience left in her as I have, gives a fake lunge and one of her earth-shaking growls.

The local dogs scatter, and the owner of the ring leader—a slightly less mangy, brown-and-black dog whose great-great-grandmother may have once had a little liaison with a Rottweiler—steps out of his wooden house and bellows in terror what I take to be, *"What, do you have a death wish? Get your stupid ass in here before I have to dig eight holes to bury all the pieces of you."*

The dogs begin to scatter long before the words are out of the owner's mouth. We do, however, notice that all the male dogs simply back off a little. They continue to follow along at a safer distance behind us. This is a bad sign. Is Rocca coming into heat? Oh my God. Please no! Our girl has irregular cycles. Very irregular. Getting her spayed would solve all these problems, but Jack is still hoping that Chesty and Rocca will produce some pups that he can place into puppy slavery with loving rich people. I decide not to think about the possibility of keeping the two dogs apart in a hotel room until I see actual blood. No blood, no problem. That's my new motto.

Back at the hotel room, I hide under the covers and dive into the black oblivion of an afternoon nap. Jack takes Chesty and goes to visit the hotel owner, Sally. In the late afternoon, we walk the dogs and then eat at a burger place owned by a guy from Alabama and his much younger Panamanian wife. The young wife cooks and cleans and waits tables. The old, fat husband shoots the shit with the *gringos* who stagger in out of the heat and humidity to enjoy a greasy taste of home. The arrangement seems to work for them, and the burgers are glorious. Unfortunately, we won't be eating any more of them as, unbeknownst to us, they have a pet cat named Paws. Paws, an orange tabby who like all cats, understands his role as king of the known universe, struts out of the kitchen and jumps up onto a chair on the other side of the restaurant from us.

Jack has the leash draped casually across his lap. Chesty leaps to his feet and is across the room in a nanosecond. The cat hesitates. I can see ol' Paws start to arch his back and do his best enraged emperor imitation, but the closer this black beast comes to him, the less Paws is thinking that standing and fighting is such a terrific idea. Deciding it's better to run and fight another day, the cat darts back to the kitchen with Chesty in hot pursuit. By the time Jack captures our cat-chasing boy, we have attracted an audience from the full length of Main Street. The cat is perched on top of the oven fan, his back arched, his orange fur sticking straight up all over his body. We are asked to never again return to the restaurant with the dogs.

I slink away with Rocca, who has watched the show with her usual expression of disdain. Jack grins as we walk down the sand street, waving at people as we go.

"Well," he says about the Alabamian owner as we come back to the hotel room. "For a good ol' boy that guy doesn't have much of a sense of humor, does he?"

SIXTEEN
IT'S BETTER THAN THE HOTEL!

THE SKY IS pouring buckets of warm rain as we move into our yellow house in Little Saigon, Bocas del Toro, Panama. Once inside the fence, the gate shut and locked, the dogs are ecstatic to be off-lead. Chesty immediately explores every inch of the yard and begins a running battle with the neighborhood buzzards. The dull-black birds are of the opinion that they were here first. Chesty, being a capitalist dog, thinks that he's paying rent now, so the yard is his. He does manage to evict two stray cats who have been bedding down in a small pile of unburnable garbage in the back corner of the yard. He roots around among the tin cans and old engine parts until he's assured himself that these invaders are gone. Rocca stays with me, and we explore the house itself.

It's an interesting floor plan. Downstairs is a large room with three sets of bunk beds, two twin beds, and a double bed. These are arranged with just enough room to walk between them. Along the walls are metal shelves with rusty coat hangers dangling. I'm thinking maybe this was a hospital at one time. What the hell are all these beds doing here?

Also downstairs is a small camp-style kitchen. There are wooden shelves with battered, blackened pots and pans and mismatched plates, glasses, and silverware, a hotplate, one of those old, round-cornered refrigerators that might turn out to be white once I remove the mold, and a cold water spigot. There's a tiny half-bath on the ground floor too, with a small sink and a toilet that, with our long *gringo* legs, we'd have to sit on sideways to use.

A voice in my head is screaming, "This is not the way I expected to live when I moved down here! Stupid! Stupid woman to have moved here at all!"

I begin to long for my lovely, wide-body refrigerator-freezer with the ice and water in the door. Why did we come here? And am I really the kind of person who needs material comforts and instant gratification? Ice and cold water at the touch of a button? It's looking more and more like I am that kind of person, yeah. And the cold-water thing. I've heated water on a stove to wash dishes in the past. While I was camping! Not in my own kitchen. Still, the yellow house is better than the hotel room. Much, much better. I need to keep telling myself this. It will be my new mantra.

Rocca and I go up the steep stairs on the outside of the house to see what we find. A nice balcony wraps around two sides of the house on the top floor. It's narrow, but shaded, and catches a *brisa fresca* or fresh breeze. Inside we discover a living room, a bathroom with a cold-water shower, and two bedrooms. One bedroom has a double bed, a small, scarred wooden desk, and the standard metal shelf equipped with coat hangers. The second bedroom has a bunk bed, a double bed, and two more metal shelves. These shelves hold a collection of well-used beach hats.

The floors are wood planking. Just like we had in the hunting cabin I remember from my childhood. The windows have no glass. They are covered instead with wooden, louvered French shutters. When we open the shutters, there's just air between us and the great outdoors. The walls are more wood planking. The furniture is old but serviceable, a little funky, but that's good. We won't have to worry about the dogs doing any damage. I mean, really, what damage could they actually do here?

"Well?" asks Jack. "What do you think?"

"It's better than the hotel," I recite.

"What the hell is with all these beds?" he wonders aloud.

We count up the number of people that could sleep here. Sixteen. Thirty if you count the hammock hooks that dot every available wall and post.

We keep exploring our new domain and find a locked storage room. Peeking in through a broken shutter, we see dismantled bed frames and two stacks of mattresses that reach from floor to ceiling. What the hell?

We drag our suitcases up the stairs and unpack. This doesn't take long as we have very few earthly possessions. Oh my God! This is what I've accumulated in fifty-five years on this planet? Two suitcases of goods, one of which contains a dwindling supply of dog food. Okay, not to panic. I'm better off here than I was in the hotel. "But," says that sly, critical voice in my head, "you're a hell of a lot worse off than you were in the large, comfortable house in Arizona you voluntarily abandoned." Stupid voice.

Jack and I collapse on the double bed in the first bedroom upstairs. The other room is slightly larger and sits at the back of the small house, but moving all the beds requires more effort than we're capable of right now. Rocca relaxes on the upstairs balcony, and Chesty continues to race around and around the yard looking for trouble. We lie on the bed and practice breathing deeply.

"So?" Jack asks. "Are you a happy girl now?"

What the hell am I going to say?

You know all those marriage manuals that tell you to always be truthful with your spouse? The ones that have those nifty little sayings like *Secrets + Fear = Unhappiness*. You know the books I'm talking about. Well, they're full of shit. The secret to a happy marriage is to know how to bend the truth into a friggin' pretzel.

"I like the fenced yard," I tell my husband. "And this is sure as hell better than the hotel!"

"Well, good," he says as he rolls me over so we can spoon. "I'm glad you like it. Now maybe you'll relax and settle down a little."

"Maybe," I answer. But I don't have high hopes.

Just as we decide to break in our new marriage bed, we hear Chesty going nutso outside. You get to know your dog's different barks. Chesty has a distinctive bark that means he's treed some prey. A cat, a buzzard, a squirrel, a gecko, a mouse, whatever. He has an entirely different bark that means he's protecting against a danger and needs back-up. This is the bark we hear. Rocca races downstairs where her growls rattle the walls. We get up and go out on the balcony to see what's going on.

The sand street in front of our new house is filled with a dozen children ranging in age from toddler to about eight years of age. The older kids wear the blue skirt or pants and white shirts that are the required school uniform around here. The little guys have on ratty shorts and mostly no tops at all. Two are so little they sport nothing but a droopy diaper. All of these beautiful, smiling children have their hands filled with rocks they have retrieved from the pile across the street at a building site and are now having a gay old time hurling them at our dogs.

Chesty has never had anything like this happen to him before. He, like me, has led a sheltered life. He loves kids and can't figure out why they are throwing rocks at him. Rocca stands back out of range, and then seeing that the little monsters aren't responding to her threats and that she can't get at them to enforce it, she turns around and retreats to the balcony.

"HEY!" I yell. "NO! *No moleste mi perros!*"

Jack takes a more direct approach. He walks downstairs and begins to open the gate to the yard. Chesty is excited now, and even Rocca has come back downstairs in the hope of being allowed to run through the little herd of tormentors, scattering them in umpteen different directions. The kids back away. The bigger ones drag the little guys with them.

"*Ustedes moleste mi perros y yo voy a libre mi perros para hace todas los niños para sus comida.*" Jack grins maliciously at the kids.

What he hopes this means is "If you bother my dogs, I'm going to turn them loose to eat all of you little pukes."

Of course, it undoubtedly means no such thing. The kids, nevertheless, get the idea and scatter. It's not that they're being bad, these kids. They really don't know any better. They've been taught from birth to throw rocks at stray dogs to keep them away. The concept of an animal having feelings or being worthy of respect is as foreign to them as the idea of washing my dishes in cold water is to me. I understand this, but I'm still pissed that they're throwing rocks at my dogs.

"After all Chesty's been through to get here," I wail to Jack. "And then to have the kids hurt him like that!"

I cry and heap guilt on myself for bringing Chesty into a situation where his innocence has been shattered.

Hey! I warned you I wasn't dealing in anything resembling emotional reality, didn't I?

"They didn't hurt him," Jack says as he checks Chesty all over for bumps or abrasions.

"Not physically!" I wail, in high-drama mode now for sure.

"Let's put the dogs in the house and see if we can find a grocery store where we can stock the cupboards a little." Jack tries to change the subject.

"Leave the dogs here?" I ask, as though he's suggested we beat them with chains.

"Sure. Why not? Maybe we'll walk uptown and see if we can get some lunch while we're out."

I know it's ridiculous to be concerned about leaving the dogs in a locked house, behind a locked gate. But, what if someone steals them? As soon as we're seen on the street, everyone in town will know that the dogs are here alone. How do I know who has the keys to this house?

Everybody on the island has met these dogs. They all know where we've moved, and they all have cell phones to call their buddies and say, "Yeah. I'm looking at the two dumb *gringos* right now here on Main Street. The dogs have got to be at the yellow house. Go for it. We'll make a fortune with those monsters at the dog fights."

Okay. So, the chance of anybody risking life and limb to the teeth of these two dogs is slim to none. But, still, it could happen. And also, what if the dogs figure out a way to get out of the house somehow? I check all the wooden shutters. They lock from the inside. So the dogs can't escape unless they chew their way out, and neither dog is that much of a chewer. Plus, it would take them two weeks of steady work to bite through the walls. All right, fine, so they're not likely to escape.

So, what exactly is it that makes me frightened to leave them? Ah, yes. That would be my ever-deepening psychosis. I decide that this is one of those times in life when I have to allow my intellect to overrule my emotions. There's a novel idea, eh?

I take a deep breath, hold Jack's hand, and we lock the dogs inside and step dogless out into the world of Bocas.

As we're locking the gate, we look around at our new neighborhood. When we were here before to see the house, our desperation to get out of Sally's hotel kept us from paying much attention to detail. That and the fact that there is no actual good neighborhood on this island. It's just a bunch of folks jumbled up together—rich, poor, destitute—that all live as neighbors in this friendly island paradise.

Yeah. I'm being sarcastic. Fear does that to me.

Now we look around the area a little. On one side of our new house are eight wooden, one-room shacks that rest on stilts. These are scattered around a lot about the size as the one we are renting. The ground around these houses is bare dirt, garbage raked neatly into small piles around which are naked children, starving dogs, and the ever-present buzzards. On the other side is a small cement house with a flower-filled yard and a woman who wears many black bras. I know this because six of them are hanging on an outside line at the moment.

Across the street is a taxi depot. A mechanic pounds on something under the hood of a Toyota pickup, and two young men wash another Toyota truck. Next to the taxi depot is a construction site. A two-story cement house is going up. Six young men haul gravel and sand from the piles out front in through the door of the house in wheelbarrows. Right now, I count seventeen children within a few feet of our new home. Most under the age of ten.

"Oh God!" I moan to Jack as I eyeball the little guys. "Poor Chesty."

"Yeah." He nods. Tact never being one of his virtues, he adds, "A herd of rock-throwing kids and a crazy mama."

Walking the few blocks to Main Street, we zigzag around the town, desperately searching for a small comfort zone where we might be able to buy a place and live happily until our next attack of insanity instigates yet another move. It's becoming increasingly clear that there really isn't any such place here. We either have to get comfortable with Bocas the way it is or leave. At the moment, neither of us seems able to do either of these things. Though the laid-back atmosphere is beginning to appeal to me, the dirt and garbage are more than I can get past on my way to acceptance.

We stop at Sally's hotel and promise to take her to dinner as a thank you for all she's done for us since we staggered into town. She laughs when we tell her that, because of all the beds, we wonder if our new rental house might have been a hospital at one time. As she explains it, Panamanians arrive at these beach houses from the mainland with sixty or so of their friends and relatives. They throw down mattresses on every available floor space, hang hammocks from every hook and post, and convince the little ones that sleeping cheek to jowl in a blanket tent is an adventure. The families come in on Friday night and party until they collapse, sleep a few hours, and start their celebration of life all over again until, at vacation's end, they drag themselves back to the boat or plane returning them to their homes and jobs in Panama City.

The concept of willingly spending time with a crowd of people is foreign to both Jack and me. We came here seeking solitude and privacy in a peaceful setting. Sally assures us that's available here, just not in Bocas Town. Which presents an obstacle. The reason the houses on all the islands that we've seen are all jumbled together like discarded children's blocks is that only a small section of each island has electricity and water.

Once you get outside that cluster of infrastructure, you're off the grid and must supply and maintain your own electrical and water supply. Sewage disposal is no problem, a plastic tank in the ground takes care of that, assuming the land isn't solid rock. Garbage is a much bigger obstacle. There are no dumps here. All garbage must be hauled off the island on a barge. Which is expensive and the reason most people just burn everything they don't use, including all manner of plastic, shredded rubber tires, and other assorted oil-based trash.

Off the grid here is not the same as off the grid in the United States. To obtain a generator, a water pump, or a part of any kind you must fly to David. And this is an island surrounded by a very salty sea, so constant maintenance and repair are a given. A round-trip ticket to David is $136, and a plane conveniently leaves three times a week. Unfortunately, the plane schedule means you must fly into David, the second-largest town in the country, do your shopping and then stay overnight in a hotel for one or two nights, depending on which day of the week a flight is returning to this island paradise.

Here's another thought. Jack's weight bumps up against 275 pounds. If we're living on the backside of an island and he has a heart attack, or his reoccurring back problem kicks up, or he gets injured in any one of four dozen ways that pop into my head without even thinking hard, how do I get him onto a boat? And once on the boat, I'd need to drive across a channel or two, depending upon what island we were living, to reach Bocas Town. There I could presumably find help getting him out of the boat and into a taxi, so that we could transport him to the airport where we would then have to hire a private plane to fly him to Panama City for treatment.

Talk about not thinking things through before we uprooted ourselves and relocated to a foreign country! Is there a prize for the most foolish people on earth? 'Cause if there is, I wanna enter. I think we've got a shot at winning big!

In the meantime, we eat lunch at one of Jack's favorite greasy spoons. Deep-fried chicken gizzards and Panamanian tortillas. Have I told you about these tortillas? First of all, forget you've ever seen those flat Mexican jobbers. A Panamanian tortilla bears no resemblance whatsoever to one of its Mexican cousins. The tortillas here are sweetened cornmeal mush, flattened between the cook's palms, and then deep fried in lard. They are as delicious as they are heart-attack inducing. Wonderful comfort food as long as you're going to be happy weighing twice your recommended weight. Of course, for a young, hard-working male, this is no problem. Lard-fried corn is a great source of fat and energy. But neither Jack nor I fit this description, so we eat these tortillas at our peril.

Except that I am having a wee little problem with my stomach. I don't seem able to keep anything in it longer than five minutes. It's my body talking to my head.

My stomach says, "Leave! Flee! Run for your life! Check the gangrene in your right arm again. I think it's just about ready to be hacked off with your handy-dandy pocket knife."

My head answers, "Not yet Goddamnit! I'm sure if I just twist this situation around for a little longer, I'll find some way to shift this boulder and save my pride and make this move be the best decision of my life. Just shut up, leave me alone. As a stomach, shouldn't you be concentrating on digestion or something?"

After lunch and a stop at the grocery store, we swing by Sally's to give her our new cell phone number. She invites us into her office, and for the first time, I notice what she has on the wall above her computer—one of those calendars featuring the United States national park system. November's picture is of a sun-dappled redwood forest. My childhood home. The place where I grew up and raised my children. Where my family still lives. Looking at the picture, I can smell the ancient forest. I don't know I'm crying until I feel the splashes of tears on my chest. It's all I can do not to reach my arm toward the image, my pointer finger extended, and moan, "Home! ET go home!"

"I'm sorry," I sniffle and say to Sally.

"Ah, honey, don't worry about it," she assures me. "I've grown to love Bocas, and I still break down in crying jags from time to time over the choice of living here. It'll get better. More and more, you'll learn to balance the good of the place with the hardship."

Jack leads me away while I swipe my hand across my runny nose. Outside, we pass an old man under a spreading tree playing an ancient acoustic guitar. A small herd of black buzzards waddle along behind us. I wonder if they too smell the rot of our hopes and dreams.

SEVENTEEN
SAND FLEAS
AND OPEN WINDOWS

N OW THAT THE immediate problem of suitable shelter has been solved, we discover more and more about Bocas del Toro. I could tell you that we begin to slowly shed our *gringo* expectations and learn to love the island life here. I've been known to stretch the truth, but not shatter it into a million tiny lies. We confront, every single day, more reasons why we must get ourselves and the dogs off these islands that we worked so hard to get to, and so we develop a new plan.

If you ever get a chance to visit Bocas del Toro in the Republic of Panama, jump at the opportunity. It's a beautiful, nearly enchanting place to visit. With plenty of money and someone else to take care of all your needs, Bocas truly is paradise. But, while it is a beautiful tourist destination, Jack and I confirm for ourselves that there is no way we want to live here.

The grocery stores are an interesting blend of Latin America, tourist shop, and Chinese apothecary. Latin American in that the shelves are stocked with tiny portions of food stuffs. You know those miniature jars of mayonnaise, mustard, and ketchup you buy for an outrageous price at a campground in the States when you don't want to drag your giant-sized jar of mayonnaise from home? That's what they have here—itty bitty containers of everything from tuna fish to milk and margarine. Same price as that campground store, too.

There's a loaf of bread at the checkout counter so you can buy one slice at a time. The cashier just opens the plastic wrapper, reaches in with her bare hands, grabs the top slice of bread, and puts it in a plastic bag for you. Processed cheese slices and eggs can be purchased on the same system. Almost every time we go in the little store down the sandy road from our place, Jack pays for a slice of bread, a plastic-wrapped slab of cheese, or an egg—enough to treat a kid or two. Our treks to the market have come to look like a slightly-crazed, pied piper parade with Jack and Chesty on point, Rocca and me close behind, followed by a ragtag band of small children. Drag position is always filled by a waddling troop of ever-hopeful black buzzards.

The grocery stores are tourist shops in that they stock supplies that locals would never buy. Diet colas, apples and grapes and other expensive, exotic fruit, beach mats, suntan lotion, postcards, and ice cream Popsicles. At first, I thought local folks probably enjoy an ice cream sandwich from time to time. I was wrong. These ice cream treats cost over two dollars each. In an economy where a good wage is seven dollars a day, sucking down a Magnum ice cream bar is the equivalent of us treating ourselves to a lobster dinner.

In lieu of store-bought ice cream, locals eat something called a "Duro." Families that have freezers and can afford to pay for the electricity to run the modern contraption post a hand-lettered sign in front of their house. These entrepreneurs sell a local popsicle made by adding a small portion of smashed, local, seasonal fruit to coconut milk. This mixture is then poured into a small plastic bag, frozen, and sold as a Duro.

The neighborhood kids love them. They untie the plastic knot on the end and push the icy treat into their mouths, dropping the emptied plastic bag wherever they happen to be standing when they've finished. The old plastic wrappers look like used condoms, complete with sticky, milky substance trapped in the tips. For a while, I looked askance at the local male population as these wrappers would fit a sadly short but amazingly thick penis.

The Asian influence is demonstrated by the fact that all the stores in the entire country, or all that I've seen in my two weeks here, are owned and operated by Chinese. Evidently some of these folks had ancestors that came over to work on the Panama Canal, and the rest have flowed across the waters to join friends and family or have been recruited by Panamanian-Chinese to work as indentured servants. It has taken me two weeks to figure out that the reason my horrible Spanish doesn't work in grocery stores is that most of the clerks speak, not Spanish, but one of a dozen or so Chinese dialects.

Along with the aforementioned miniature jars of condiments, these stores also stock herbal medicines—dried roots and insects—along with dozens of soaps and lotions to assist the buyer with anything from casting a love spell to relieving a mosquito bite itch. Judging by the number of remedies that include ground pig tusks and liquefied bull penis, Chinese men require more assistance than is normal to achieve a hard-on.

These shops all have very narrow aisles and shelves stocked using a system I have not yet deciphered. At the market closest to us, coffee is scattered about the store in six different locations, though the tea is all together behind the counter. After finding tiny bags of sugar, I'm left to wander two aisles over to find the flour. Butter is in two different refrigerator units and is purchased by the half-cube. Eggs are not refrigerated and are bought individually and, when purchased, placed loose in a plastic bag. The meat counter is in the back, and while I am just going to assume that the meat is refrigerated where it's stored, once the bloody flesh gets to the open case, it's on its own in the heat. A girl of about ten usually does her best to fan away the flies with a swatter gooped with her latest kills.

I have decided to become a vegetarian.

There are no alternatives to these types of markets. Well, that's not quite true. There is one Gourmet Grocery store run by a woman from the States. Unfortunately, the prices in this store are prohibitive for anything other than the occasional treat to keep myself from starving on the local fare. There are fish markets, but seafood is also high-priced. There are two reasons for this. First, the fishermen have figured out that they can make a lot more money taking tourists out for snorkeling and island-hopping excursions than they can possibly earn fishing.

Second, the remaining fishermen sell to the tourist restaurants that line the bay for a higher price than they can get from locals or cheapskate *gringos* like Jack and me.

Coming from the States, I have taken for granted the concept that shopping is fun. I grew up with wide aisles lined with products displayed in an eye-catching manner. I've grown accustomed to choosing between seventeen brands of mustard, eighty-two specialized shampoos, and eleven types of white flour. Does anyone really need all these choices? Certainly not. Do I miss not having them? You betcha.

Dog food is another challenge down here. Our dogs have never eaten corn in their lives. Until now. Dogs don't digest corn any better than people, plus many canines are allergic to this filler. If you've just jumped up and run to check the ingredient list on your expensive and veterinarian recommended Science Diet or the Purina HiPro that the commercials have promised you is used by all the top breeders and that you have paid big bucks to feed to your Brutus or Fifi, you will see that the second or third ingredient is corn. Regardless of what you've been told by the people selling this food, it's not good for Brutus or Fifi, and it may be doing harm to your best friend.

Our dogs have always eaten a diet free of lamb, rice, and corn. No such thing is available down here. Here, there are two brands of dog food. Both have *maíz* listed as the first ingredient, followed by, not meat, but meat by-products, meaning it's what gets swept up off the floor each day at the end of the butchering, after they make the hotdogs. To these remains, the makers of doggie kibble add the noses, hooves, and tails that are too disgusting even to be transformed into Spam.

This is not a food we want to feed our big babies. However, we must work with the options available. We decide to feed them the best of the two bad kibble choices and to supplement with cooked meat and the vitamins and flax we brought with us. Once again, not the end of the known world, but not a solution with which we're totally comfortable either. Hopefully we'll get lucky and neither dog will develop a corn allergy.

The Little Saigon section of Bocas lies along a curve of pale brown bay water known as Big Creek. The water is shallow within this nearly complete circle of land. It's one of those bocas or mouths for which these islands are named. The Caribbean glints slate-blue out beyond the stretching fingers of the two peninsulas that come within a few hundred yards of touching. The less attractive color and texture of the bay water is due to the mangroves that line the banks and to the slightly muddy bottom. The shore is the same mix of sand and mud, inundated with garbage dropped by beachgoers or returned by Mother Ocean from, more or less, where it originated.

People keep saying to us, "Oh, you live on Big Creek. How lucky for you. That's the nicest beach on the island."

No kidding? This strikes me as analogous to saying, "That is the warmest town in the Arctic," or "You have the best home in the roadside trailer park." I mean, I'm happy for them and all, but I want to ask, "Have you traveled much? Do you know what lies beyond walking distance of the place where you were born?" Okay. That's snotty. I know. But seriously folks, Big Creek is by no stretch of the imagination a nice beach.

Yet, once again, we try to convince ourselves we're in paradise. We take the dogs and go, early in the morning, to beachcomb along the curve of Big Creek beach. We don't find any shells. We do discover, and fairly quickly, why we're the only people here to watch the sunrise. Pretty much the exact instant the sun peaks above the horizon line and begins its daily blessing of the land, the sand fleas wake up, rub their gritty little eyes, and attack in hordes. We swat, cuss, and finally, run for our lives.

My flea-avoidance strategy is to rush into the water and squat down in the shallow brown liquid so that only my head is exposed. The tiny teeth with wings continue to bite my face, neck, and head, but at least I'm saving my arms and legs. I now discover that Rocca isn't much of a water dog. Swimming doesn't appear to be her strong suit. She runs along in the water with the leash stretched tight as close to the shore as she can get while I duck walk through the murky bay telling myself that these island waters are not known for sharks.

Jack takes a different approach. He runs full speed along the shore, leaps over flotsam, jumps jetsam, and streaks through the garbage while he flaps at his arms and legs. He bellows and cusses and attempts to intimidate with foul threats to annihilate the whole stinking species. Chesty hasn't had this much fun for weeks. He runs and jumps and grabs Jack's shoes with his mouth, causing Jack's getaway to be punctuated with near falls and additional cusses directed at his helpful "service" dog.

By the time we make it off the beach, we have somewhere between two and three hundred bug bites each. The dogs, however, appear to have gotten the worst of it. The bitey-bugs hide in their fur and continue to cause misery. We trot to the house and rush in the gate to bathe both dogs. Thirty minutes later, we haven't obliterated the sand fleas, but the damn bugs are sopping wet, soapy, and on the retreat. We all haul our bitten bodies up the stairs, throw ourselves on and around the bed, and turn on the air conditioning to ease the itching.

"Well, hey," says Jack, "that was really fun. Wanna do it all again tomorrow morning?"

Our bed has a window over its head and another on the wall to the left. The one on the left opens to the roof of the house where an extra four dozen mattresses are stored. Both windows are covered in French louvers, no glass. Once the shutters are swung open, there's nothing to separate us from the humid outdoors. Just open air. The window at the head of our bed looks out onto the street that runs in front of the house. It's a two-story drop from this window to the sparse grass in the yard below. I want to keep this window closed at all times as I'm in my usual obsessive worry mode. I envision one of the dogs leaping out the window and falling to the earth in a broken heap.

Seriously, actual nightmare visions of the fall are like slow motion slides in my head.

"They're not going to jump out that window!" Jack tells me and I translate as, "I am the all-powerful Oz. I can accurately predict the future using my giant male brain."

Our third day in the house, Jack goes up town accompanied by Chesty. Rocca and I stay home where I plan to search the internet for a house in the States we can pay cash for with the money we have from the sale of our home in Arizona. So far, I've come up with Cloudcroft, New Mexico, where it snows nine and a half months a year and Whitesville, Louisiana where we will be asked to have a blood test proving our ancestry before being admitted to the compound.

I walk Jack to the gate so that I can lock it behind him, leaving Rocca in the house so she can't slip out the gate and go with them. Rocca hates to be the dog left behind.

As Jack and Chesty and I start down the stairs, I notice the window over the bed is open.

"Wait!" I say. "Just let me run back inside and shut the window, and then I'll come back down and lock the gate."

"You do whatever you have to do," Jack tells me in the exasperated voice of a man who has dealt too long with a crazy woman. "I'm going. You can come back down and lock the gate."

I get inside the house just in time to see Rocca launch herself out the second story window. My scream is loud enough to stun a billy goat. Rocca, either because of the scream or, more likely, because she realizes that she is throwing herself into mid-air, arches her body backward, does a twisted flip, and manages to end up with the heavier back end of her body inside the house. Someone is still screaming as I grab her collar and yank her teetering front end back inside.

From the window, I glare down and give Jack a look that could freeze molten lava.

"See." He grins broadly. "I told you she wouldn't jump out that window."

Before I can close and lock the window and make it back down the stairs, he and Chesty have disappeared. They take a different route than usual to go up town, too. I can't find them anywhere, and I look for thirty minutes until the flames coming out my ears have cooled to smoke, and I begin to worry about Rocca, who was left locked in the house.

Just before dark, Jack and Chesty return to the house with take-out pizza and that faux-macho manner common to all males who have pissed off a female of pretty much any species. Really, they look like deer in headlights. Rocca and I are curled up on the bed together. She has her head on my shoulder and is either shook up by her near miss, or she's using my concern to get all the attention she can handle. Probably the latter, but I prefer to think the former.

Once we've had our pizza, I decide not to bring up Rocca almost dying since Jack isn't going to listen to me about a "dangerous situation in our midst."

Yeah. Right. No reason at all to say, "I told you so, you arrogant jackass." Ah...
yeah. But if you believe that's the last he heard of the incident, I have a hell of
a deal on an island paradise in the southern Caribbean that I'd be willing to
let you have at a not-to-be-missed bargain price.

EIGHTEEN
I DEVELOP A LIST AND
THE BAND PLAYS ON

THE KIDS IN the neighborhood are a constant source of entertainment for me. I do mean constant, and I don't necessarily mean clap my hands and jump for joy entertainment. They're up before the chickens and goats in the morning, and when I close my eyes at 10 o'clock or so in the evening, they're still running the streets in ragtag gangs. We've solved the rock throwing by never letting the dogs outside alone. I bring the dogs inside and out of range as soon as I see the first charmer bend over to retrieve a missile. One little guy has a boulder too big for him to throw that someone has tied on a length of knotted rope. He drags this stone along behind him everywhere like a reluctant pet.

In the mornings, the street is overflowing with these children. They sweep the dirt road with palm branches and wage war amongst themselves using swords of pilfered rebar and jagged shovel handles. Evidently, that old mother's warning, "you'll put your eye out with that thing," doesn't work cross-culturally. These kids are all physically whole despite several hours each day spent thrusting whatever sharp implement they can scour from the jungle or construction site across the street into the faces of their friends and cohorts.

Their newest game causes me to utter an oath ending with the words, "What fresh hell is this?" These clever children have formed a band. Two little boys beat on plastic gallon jugs hung around their necks with dirty string. One employs an elbowed length of driftwood as a drum stick, and the other uses a bent butter knife. The two little girls in the gang are evidently not allowed to, or don't care to, play an instrument. They are the majorettes and lead the band. These wannabe beauty queens carry bent lengths of metal pipe which they toss over their heads with abandon, drop, and retrieve to twirl again.

The toddler from the stilted house that pushes up against the fence line of our place wears his usual droopy diaper and hammers on a slightly dented gallon tin can using two mismatched curtain rods. Three preschoolers have rock-and-nail-filled aluminum beer cans tied together with beachcombed fishing line. These noisemakers bump and drag along the road as the little guys bring up the near-end of the parade.

At the tail end of the ragtag line marches Chesty's nemesis—the little guy with the crooked grin and faded purple shorts, the one who cannot resist chucking rocks at the dogs no matter the threat of reprisal from their *gringo* owners. From the taxi depot across the road, this little beach rat has stolen two smashed hubcaps which he has fitted with coconut husk-wrapped wire handholds. He clangs and bangs his homemade cymbals and, because he's just that kind of little boy, sings some Panamanian martial song at the top of his lungs. Gee, he's a live wire, ain't he?

On the third day of this ongoing performance, another little boy finds a way to join in the parade. He hasn't salvaged an instrument, but he struts along with the majorettes, leading the billy goat which is usually staked in a nearby empty lot. The child has tied a yellow bow of plastic police tape around the animal's horns, and dragging the goat by the hemp rope it is usually staked with, this ingenious little guy leads the whole shebang. He sashays down the road, gestures to the onlookers with a beauty pageant wave, and smiles just like the soap opera stars on TV.

We are bombarded with this production from dawn to midnight. Do these children ever sleep? Do they nap in shifts? They are as cute as they can be. For the first fifteen minutes each morning. By noon, I'm no longer amused by their antics, and when 10:00 p.m. approaches, I understand why they wouldn't allow me to bring a handgun into the country.

Actually, the band does take a break each day at about 1:00 p.m. when they all troop to the beach and splash in the brown bay. The older ones watch the younger ones. Presumably. None of them have drowned since we've been here, anyway. The bay is shallow, and there are usually adults there as well. This is a culture that understands the idea that it takes a village to raise a child.

This child-rearing concept is graphically demonstrated when a local maid finds a stash of child pornography in her *gringo* employer's dresser drawer. It's noted by locals that this same man often invites young, male children into his home to play games on his computer and for special food treats like ice cream and potato chips. The locals talk with the children who are the special friends of this middle-aged pedophile. Two days later, the maid finds the guy naked and seated at his computer, child porn spread out around him. His decapitated head is now in his lap performing a function that, if possible when he was alive, might have saved him a tremendous amount of trouble and actually prevented his death.

Clearly, this is a community that protects its children. No charges are filed. The man's possessions disappear into the populous, and life goes on as before. So I suppose these folks wouldn't take kindly to me strangling one of the little rock-chucking noise-makers either.

We continue to look for a place to buy, but we're gradually, reluctantly coming to terms with the reality of Bocas real estate. The only homes where we might be able to live semi-comfortably are ten times what we can afford, and the properties we can afford require more energy and work than we possess these days. Maybe more of both than we ever had, even in our physical prime. So, we search the World Wide Web looking for alternatives. We could go back to the States and buy in rural Tennessee or Georgia. Both of those areas offer beautiful mountain land at affordable prices. But neither of us has ever lived where it snows or stays cold for months at a time. We know from cruel experience that wet and cold places are going to make Jack ache in every one of the sixty-six spots where shrapnel is still embedded in his body.

Finally, like two blind mice who accidentally stumble their way out of a complex maze, we happen to look at other areas in Panama. The

Pacific coast, on the other side of this narrow country, is where the bulk of foreigners live. I wonder why that is? We check it out, and as near as we can determine, the reason for the appeal of this area is two-fold. First of all, from the beginning, nearly every single foreigner who ever set foot in this country lived in Panama City. Most of them came because of the canal, which lies at the entrance to the capital on the Pacific side and flows to Colón on the Atlantic side. English is spoken by enough people here that you can get by without hiring a private translator.

Second of all, Panama City has grown into a modern skyscraper-lined mega-capital, dominated by the banking industry which succors the gambling industry, as well as real estate developers. Panamanians brag that they can find anything in Panama City—you just have to know where to look and whom to ask. This tiny Central American country has one of the most beautiful and modern capitals in the world. Its people are rightfully proud of it, even as they seek respite from the city's noise and pollution at their country houses, usually no more than an hour's drive from the faster-paced city.

Therefore, the infrastructure north of the city for one hundred kilometers, more or less, is excellent. The roads are good. Well, the main roads are relatively good. Once you turn off the Pan-American Highway, you'll be bumping along for a while until you reach your destination, unless your country home is in one of the dozens of gated communities hidden along this coast. We originally had no interest whatsoever in living in a gated community. However, as I look out the window from where I sit at our computer and watch the local band make yet another loop along the road, while I smell the burning plastic and rubber coming from umpteen small garbage fires in the yards around us, I begin to waver just a bit on this decision.

We call RE/MAX in the city. Remember Arie, our buddy who picked us up at the airport when we arrived and transported us and our two huge and disturbingly naughty dogs to the hotel in the city? The guy who, after meeting us, had an unexpected appointment out of the country and didn't expect to be back in the foreseeable future? We call him, and lo and behold, he's returned from his surprise expedition out of cell phone reach and answers his phone. We explain that we made it to Bocas, don't like this particular paradise, and are now thinking of looking for a place on the Pacific coast.

Which, by the way, is what Arie recommended from the beginning.

"Ah." Jack has Arie on speaker phone. *"Sadly, I am leaving the country again very soon. Before you could get here from the islands, for sure I will be gone. But I have two associates who would be delighted to help you in your search for a home here on the Pacific coast."*

"Okay. That sounds good," Jack tells him. "I'm thinking of flying into the city tomorrow to start looking for something to buy. Can someone meet me at the airport?"

"Ah, yes. This is no problem," Arie says with a glee in his voice that makes me wonder what these associates of his have done to piss him off. *"Leo and Annabella. They both speak excellent English and will be happy to pick you up and drive you around to look at homes here. Let me give you their cell phone numbers. That way you will be able to call them directly and have no need to contact me."* He hesitates for a moment, perhaps hearing how that last bit sounded, and adds, *"This dealing with them will be much better for you. More convenient. They will be available to you twenty-four hours a day until they find a place for you."*

As we hang up, I'm pretty sure I hear him give a tremendous sigh of relief followed by an evil laugh.

We call Leo and Annabella who ask us to give them a few days to get properties lined up for Jack to see. We don't quite get this. How complicated is it to pull up the multiple listings on their computers and find houses that fall within the parameters we've given them?

This is the list for our new home that I compile for Jack to take with him on his house-shopping trip. I, of course, will be staying here on Bocas with the dogs.

The house must be:

1) Close to a hospital. A real hospital with doctors who have been educated in medical school, not by a local herb-toting shaman. A hospital with an understanding of the link between cleanliness and germs. We once

saw a feral cat followed by a very mangy stray dog wander through an operating room in rural Mexico. I know Panama isn't Mexico, but rural is rural, and I'd like to avoid treatment at such a place.

2) Reliable electricity, water, sewage, and garbage removal.

3) A fenced yard for the dogs or a way to put up a secure perimeter.

4) The ability to buy my meat secured under plastic or at the very least, from a refrigerated showcase. No way am I living where they hack off a chunk of meat with a machete from a steer hanging in a back alley. Again, been there, done that, do not intend to buy the T-shirt.

5) The property has to be beautiful and close to someplace I can walk in the woods or jungle or along a beach.

"No problem," says Leo when he hears this list. "Just give me until Monday of next week, and I will have many places to show you that satisfy all these requirements and are within your price range. Trust me. You will be okay. We will find you a beautiful home that you will love."

We don't believe him for one second. Still, I'm a little more hopeful than I was an hour ago.

NINETEEN
CHESTY FALLS ILL AND JACK AND I HIT BEDROCK

L IKE MANY DOG owners who are screwy about their pets, we have many nicknames for Chesty and Rocca. Chesty is Chesty Westy, Chesty Rooney Looney Tuney, Buddy Bud Bud, and when he's really messed up, Chesty Puller Jones. Rocca's aliases include Roccitey Rocc, Roccsey, and Jack's name for her when she's been horribly bad, Big Black Bitch.

I'm sure you've already picked up on the fact that political correctness is a lost concept with Jack.

This morning I sip coffee, stare blankly at the taxi depot across the dirt path, and notice that Chesty looks sad. If you have a dog that you love, you will understand this observation. If not, you've probably already stopped reading this tale so I've no need to explain it to you.

"Hey, Chesty Rooney, Looney Tuney," I sing to him. "What's goin' on, Buddy Bud Bud? How come you're not chasing buzzards and pissing everywhere a cat prowled last night to cover that stinky *gato* scent?"

Chesty glances up at me but doesn't lift his head from the wooden floor of the balcony. This is another bad sign. Calling him by these pet names always means I'm looking to play with my boy and play is something Chesty has never been known to turn down. I kneel beside him and pet his wrinkled face. He feels hot. Running my hands along his body and legs, I check for problems. When my hand touches his side, he whines and winces under my touch. Probing gently, I discover a bump where he slammed into the boat seat on our trip over from the mainland. Or possibly from our boat ride to Bastimentos Island with the short shorts-wearing realtor.

Whichever time it happened, our boy's in need of medical attention. The tropics isn't a good place to run a fever or to have an infection. I call Sally and ask for the number of the local veterinarian. There is no such thing. The only vet within a hundred miles has an office on the mainland. Sally recommends that we phone this vet and see if we need to transport Chesty to him or if he can possibly come to us after regular office hours. I call the vet and stumble through an explanation in broken Spanish. This attempt at communication is unsuccessful.

I call Sally again and ask if her assistant, who is bilingual, can call the vet for us and explain our situation.

"Yes, yes," says Camelia, Sally's beautiful, young, black assistant. "I will do this for you, no problem."

Camelia calls back an hour later to say that the vet will come from the mainland by boat tonight. He will be on the island by 7:00 and will pick Camelia up at the hotel. Then, the two of them will take a taxi to our house. We will be expected to pay for his boat ride over, his taxi, to feed him dinner, and put him up for the night at our house. This, plus his cost for the visit, will be thirty-two dollars.

All day, we try to get Chesty to drink water. He's not interested. He gets hotter and more listless as each hour passes. We keep him in the house, on the bed with the air conditioning running. Jack walks uptown to visit with Sally and the local group of *gringos* who congregate at her hotel. He returns to tell me that these helpful folks all say dogs brought down from the States rarely live a year once they get to Panama. The tropics have a whole different group of bacteria and biting bugs. Dogs from cooler climes have no natural immunity to these new diseases and threats.

"That doesn't seem right," I insist to Jack when he relays this information to me. "Why wouldn't that be the same for people immigrating down here?"

"Maybe it is," he tells me seriously.

By afternoon, a bad squall has blown in, and there's a question of whether the veterinarian will be able to come tonight at all. I have spent the day sitting next to Chesty Westy, stroking his head. Jack is on the internet, frantically trying to find Pacific coast houses to investigate once he gets to Panama City. Rocca is definitely coming into heat and is frustrated that her lovely scent isn't getting the expected reaction from her normally big, strong, enthusiastic boyfriend.

The vet finally gets to the house just after 9:00 p.m. with tales of a bad channel crossing. He only blanches for a moment when he sees the size of the dogs. We let Rocca make friends with him once she's done her growling intimidation bit and we've assured her the vet, his young male assistant, and Camelia are friends. Then, our big-boned girl wiggles her butt and takes as much attention as they're willing to provide. Once the vet is reassured that these dogs aren't going to eat him whole, I take Rocca into the second bedroom. Jack leads the vet next door into our room where Chesty is stretched limply on the bed.

The walls in this house are thin wood so I can clearly hear everything that's going on in the next room. I don't leave Rocca alone in this second room and return to be part of the examination for two reasons. Rocca is very likely to bark and raise holy hell as soon as she hears the first whine from Chesty, and I would project worry and fear to my boy, and that's the last thing he needs while being examined and treated.

I hear Chesty cry. So does Rocca. It takes some comforting, but she eventually calms down.

By the time Rocca has stopped trying to get out of the room and to her man, I hear Camelia translating for the vet.

"He says it is a very bad abscess. He's going to give the dog fluids in an IV and a very powerful shot of antibiotics. We will wait then to see if the dog has survived the night. In the morning, if all goes well, he will give your dog another shot and leave several more with you to administer. Once the dog is strong enough to move, you will need to transport him to the veterinarian's office on the mainland for surgery to lance the abscess."

I'm not sure my heart actually stops as these words reach me through the wall, but it sure as hell feels like it.

The idea that our decision to come down here has killed our dog keeps roaring through my head, blotting out any hope of a good ending here. Well, pretty much blotting out any trace of any good sense on my part at all. I need to come out of the bedroom now and make dinner for the vet who has undergone a terrible boat ride just to get here. I am very grateful to the man for coming and for treating my dog, but now I just want to go lie next to Chesty and will him to get better. To not die so that Rocca, Jack, and I, if we ever get off this frigging rain-soaked island, don't have to leave our boy behind.

As soon as I step out of the second bedroom with Rocca, Jack takes one look at my face and says, "You go in with Chesty. I'll handle Rocca and figure out dinner for the vet and his assistant."

There are moments in a marriage, often in the depth of some hellish crevice filled with seemingly insurmountable obstacles, when an action or even a look from your marriage partner mysteriously begins the process of freeing you from the death-spiral of your relationship. A moment when, having hit bedrock, the two of you glimpse the power that brought you together in the first place. This is one of those moments.

Before I go to Chesty, I stumble to Jack. We cling together, feeling each other's hearts beating in our chests, knowing that, no matter what happens now, we'll be all right. We have each other, and all the rest is, as Jack says, gravy.

Just after midnight, the vet removes the glucose drip and goes to bed in the downstairs room. No shortage of beds to choose from down there, and all of them are made up with sheets and pillows. Less than an hour later, Chesty gets to his feet, wags his stubby tail in a slow circle, and lets me know he needs to go out to pee. I try to get him to pee on the corner of the upstairs balcony, but he's had too much training to do any such thing. The dog and I make our way slowly downstairs where he's wobbly on his pins but manages to lift his leg and pee.

Back upstairs, he drinks water from his bowl, scratches at the door to the other bedroom where Rocca and Jack are sleeping, and then gives up and comes back to bed with me in the air-conditioned room. Both of us wake the next morning at 5:30 when the vet comes back to check on his patient.

Chesty eases off the bed and is standing by the time the veterinarian is in the room. I explain that the dog drank water last night and that he peed. The vet is amazed. He gives Chesty a second shot of antibiotics, leaves five more shots with Jack, and says, as near as we can decipher, that if we can keep him drinking water, he should be strong enough in three days to travel to the mainland for surgery.

We thank the vet profusely. Jack gives him the forty-seven dollars that he asks for his services and the medication, then tips him another twenty dollars, and the traveling vet is on his way to catch a boat for the forty-minute ride across the channel to open his mainland office for a day's work. By noon, Chesty is itching to go up and down the stairs to chase the buzzards from his domain. He drinks two bowls of water and begins to notice that Rocca is developing a very interesting scent. We keep him on a lead and only allow him down the stairs to pee. We decide to give him brown rice and hamburger to eat rather than the horrible dog food we've found on the island. This is no time to discover whether or not he has an allergy to corn.

Chesty has always been a picky eater. He takes one kibble at a time out of his bowl, chews it a dozen times before swallowing, and he eats little snacks all day long. This eating habit has kept him bone thin and rock hard and protected him from bloat. Big chested dogs are susceptible to this affliction when they overeat, and the food then swells in their stomachs causing their intestines to twist. It normally kills the dog, so we've always encouraged Chesty's modest manner of eating. But now, we'd be happier if he ate a little more at each setting. Rocca, on the other hand, is delighted with her new food. She gulps down as much rice and hamburger as we put in front of her and then has to be restrained from stealing the food from Chesty's bowl.

Three days later, it's obvious that Chesty's going to be okay. The knot on his side is gone. It's not even sore to the touch. When we have Camelia call the vet and tell him this, he says he will come across tonight to check for himself and to make arrangements to bring Chesty over for surgery.

By late afternoon, palms rattle and coconuts crash onto tin roofs as the rain falls in sideways sheets of silver. Nobody is going to be crossing the channel tonight to come to this island. Two days later, on Sunday afternoon, the vet makes it over. He examines Chesty and agrees with us that he doesn't need the surgery after all. The antibiotics did the trick. Thank you, Jesus, Buddha, Saint Francis, and all the dog-loving deities in the heavens above.

Jack leaves the next morning for Panama City. He's found a house on a real estate website he wants to take a look at. We've been on the phone enough now with Leo and Annabella that we finally understand that there is no multiple listing service in this country. Every realtor has his or her own list of properties. There is some overlap, as no one signs an exclusive agreement with a salesperson to sell their property, but basically, the business is cutthroat with almost no cooperation between agents. When Leo calls the listing agent to ask about the house Jack has seen and likes the look of, they won't give him any information on its location or on its current owner.

Jack buys me a cellphone so he can call and tell me about the houses he's seeing as he's looking at them. In addition to finding us a house, when he returns to Bocas, he's going to bring back a large dog crate. We can think of no other way to keep Chesty away from Rocca once she's ready to breed. The dogs will have to take turns being crated. Finding a place to live in a foreign country while Rocca is pregnant is more than I can handle and would be terribly hard on our girl. We're hoping Jack makes it back from the city before Rocca is presenting her backside to her boy.

Boy, oh boy, this adventure just keeps getting better and better, doesn't it?

TWENTY
TINY FROGS, GIANT STORMS, AND JACK FINDS A HOUSE

I'M AT THE *Albrook International Airport. Leo and Annabella are both right here, and we're leaving to go and look at houses."*

I strain to hear Jack's first phone call from the Pacific coast as a monster storm slams into Bocas. Palm fronds rattle in frenzy. Falling coconuts, thank you Jesus, have run the marching band indoors. The dogs and I are holed up in the house. Half-naked kids peek from the doorless entries of the little, wooden stilt houses next door. Occasionally, one of the children can't resist his musical leanings, and I hear a few drum beats or the sound of cymbals clashing. This is followed by loud, rapid-fire Spanish in an irritated female voice common to mothers the world over.

"I'm gonna like working with these two!" my absent husband enthuses over the phone.

"Annabella is young and pretty?" I ask.

"Very much so," Jack replies. *"Gotta go. We're headed for some breakfast and then a house tour."*

Do I know my husband or what?

I'm reading a long, boring book about the British Empire I got from Sally. One of her guests left it. Who brings a book about England to Central America? I won't tell you the title, but the ending is already clear. The world changes, and Britain loses the empire to the new kid on the block. I'm on page 238 now with only 452 pages to go. It passes the time, so I keep reading.

From time to time, every half hour or so, I check my email to see if any of the people I've been emailing five times a day have taken pity on me and answered my pleas for comfort and succor. My friend Mona humors me, and we write back and forth all day. I know more about her daily life now than I did when I lived next door. We are in the middle of a four-paragraph chat about our morning coffee—what brand, what kind of creamer, which cup we're drinking it from, how hot we prefer it to be—when, in answer no doubt to Mona's prayers, Jack calls again.

"I'm in someplace called Chame looking at a house they want sixty-seven thousand dollars for. It's pretty run-down and right on the highway, but there is a fenced yard, and we could pay cash."

"Okay. It doesn't sound like you're too impressed with this place."

"It's not what we want," he tells me. *"I just wanted to check in and let you know we're looking."*

The dogs and I decide to take another nap. I'm in the middle of the bed with Rocca on one side and Chesty on the other. The two of them fuss at each other like an old married couple until they're happy with their positions. Chesty ends up curled in a ball near the foot of the bed, and Rocca sprawls out on the opposite side with her head on the pillows and her feet pushed out as far as she can stretch them, claiming the maximum amount of space. I wedge myself in between them and hide from the world.

"The rain on the metal roof sounds nice, huh?" I ask the dogs.

Chesty circles his tail once. Rocca merely shifts her position and grunts. That's more of a response than I usually get from Jack when I make such obvious comments, so I'm happy for the input.

I dream of sitting at a table in a house I've never seen before but which is obviously mine. My three sons are with me, and we talk about something of interest to all of us. In reality, I'm not sure what that would be, but this is my dream, and here we're content to share our opinions and enjoy each other's company. Mona arrives and the two of us enthrall the boys with how we like to drink our coffee when the ringing of my little cell phone throws me back into reality.

"Hello," I mumble, still half asleep.

"I found our house!" Jack shouts happily into my ear.

"Okay." I'm coming awake now, but part of me is still hoping to get back to that imaginary kitchen table where my biggest concern was whether to use Almond Mocha or White Chocolate Creamer. "Where are you? Where's the house?"

"We're in San Carlos, and I'm standing in the front yard of the place. It looks like a park. Five acres. There are avocado trees. Orange trees. Grapefruit. Mahogany. A bunch of fruit trees that I've never heard of and a lot of flowering trees that are supposed to have yellow or pink blooms."

"Okay. Where's San Carlos?"

"On the beach, just over an hour from the city. The house is just off the highway, up against the foothills of a little mountain range. Walking distance to the beach and a nice river."

"Sounds really nice! What's the house like?"

"You gotta come and see it! It's small with a huge outdoor living area and a deep porch in front. There's a separate building with a good-sized guest suite that has a kitchen and a big bathroom. Then, I'm walking around here now, here's a bathroom with an outside entrance. What? Annabella says this is the guest bath. Jeez, here's another bedroom with its own bathroom."

"How big is this place?"

"Big. Two garages. Two big bodegas. This building I'm in now looks like a hardware store. Tools hung on racks, extra electrical supplies. There's even two shelves of sorted screws and bolts and nails!"

"So you like this place?"

"Yeah. Oh my God! Here's another whole house with two bedrooms and a bath in the middle."

"How much do they want for it?" I ask. No sense getting all excited if the place is way out of our price range.

"One hundred sixty-seven thousand dollars. I'd offer them one hundred fifty thousand dollars. We'd have to get a small bank loan to cover it, but Leo and Annabella don't think that would be a problem."

"The sounds wonderful. The yard is fenced?"

"Oh, yeah! Cement footer with a cyclone fence. There's a German Shepherd that lives here now, so it's dog proof."

"Okay. That's really good. Where's the nearest grocery store?"

"Another good thing. There's a Reyes Supermarket ten minutes away and a hospital in San Carlos, two minutes from the house on paved road all the way."

"It sounds too good to be true."

"It does, but I'm standing here looking at it. I think I'm going to make them the offer. There's no point in looking at anything else. This is what we want."

"All right. I'll come over next week to see it. Otherwise, if there's anything wrong, I'm going to blame you. And you know there'll be something wrong."

"I don't know what it would be, but yes, I want you to see the place. I think our luck is finally turning, baby."

He is almost right about that.

Just after 2:00 p.m. the rain slacks up a bit, and I take the dogs downstairs to pee and feed the buzzards. Here, there's no need to pick up and remove the daily accruement of dog shit. The leathery black vultures come each dawn and dine on the offerings. A great deal. Not only do I not have to clean up after the dogs, but Chesty gets to chase away the sewage removal crew each morning.

Today, the heavy rain has delayed the buzzards, and Chesty races downstairs to establish his dominion over his territory. Rocca hunkers down, slinks out into the rain, squats, and immediately lumbers back under the porch and looks up at me to ask when we can go back to the nice, cozy bed. Chesty has disappeared around the back of the house.

I go back upstairs and peek off the top balcony to see what he's up to back there while I stay dry under the porch. There's something hopping in the wet grass that has captured his attention. I race back downstairs. Bocas is the home of brightly colored poison dart frogs. Whatever this critter in the wet grass is, I'm not taking any chances. It turns out to be an innocuous-looking, gray, tree frog. I don't think it's poisonous, but just to be on safe side, I catch it in a paper towel and turn it loose over the fence where I hope it will live happily ever after, away from my dogs.

We go back inside where, just in case, I wash my hands for about ten minutes. There's no hot water so I trust the soap, cold water, and brisk rubbing on a towel will suffice to remove any possible toxins. I check

Chesty's mouth. There's no foaming, so I guess Bocas has plain old ordinary, non-poisonous frogs in addition to the more colorful toxic ones. The dogs arrange themselves again on the bed, and I go back to reading my sleep-inducing book.

By dark, the pounding rain has slowed to a light drizzle. The wind still roars, and coconuts still crash periodically onto the roof, but I figure this is my best chance to get the dogs back outside again for a bathroom break and a little exercise before we turn in for the night. When I make the suggestion, Rocca raises her elephant-sized head from the bed and rolls her eyes, making her wishes to remain in bed clear as a bell. I pull rank and insist she come with me downstairs to stretch her legs.

Chesty isn't interested in going outside, either. Which is odd. Chesty is always interested in cruising his property and sniffing out intruders. Rocca and I go on downstairs. I figure Chesty will join us as soon as he hears Rocca in the yard. When he doesn't, I go back up to check on him. He hasn't moved from his place at the foot of the bed. His nose isn't hot, but his eyes seem glassy. Of course, my imagination has been working overtime here lately, so maybe the dog just doesn't want to go outside in the rain and risk getting hit on the head by a falling coconut. Still, his behavior is decidedly odd.

Downstairs, I hear the low rumble from Rocca which tells me that we are about to have a night-time serenade by our little rock-chucking band of hooligans. She plods her way up the stairs, emitting a low growl at each step. All this should cause Chesty to leap from the bed, race down the stairs, and thunder along the fence line, barking a warning at the band. He does no such thing. He doesn't even raise his head from the bed when Rocca returns, still grumbling, and climbs over the top of him to get to her spot on the pillows.

Now, I'm really worried. I sit next to him and stroke his head while he moans. When Jack calls from his hotel in the city, I tell him I think there's something wrong with Chesty.

"Does he have a fever?"

"No. I don't think so."

"He's probably just depressed that I'm not there," Jack says, ever the center of our little universe. *"What's he doing?"*

"He's just sleeping on the bed. I've been petting him for the last couple of hours, and he doesn't respond to anything. Not even the little rock-throwing pukes get a rise out of him."

"Stop petting him. You're nervous about being there alone, and you're communicating that to the dog. You're making him anxious. Leave him alone. If he's not better in the morning, you can call the vet."

"I'm thinking of calling the vet now."

"And tell him what? That the dog seems depressed so can he make a boat trip over in bad weather to see if he can give him doggy Prozac?"

I laugh then. I bet they have doggy Prozac. We could get some if we lived in California.

"Okay. Okay. I get it. I'll stop worrying about the dog," I lie. "So, any more news on the house in San Carlos?"

"I wondered when you'd ask. Yeah. I offered them one hundred fifty thousand dollars. They countered with one hundred sixty thousand. I re-offered one hundred fifty-five thousand and they took it."

"Really?"

"Yeah. We should be moved in within a few weeks."

"I can't wait to see it!"

"I'll be home tomorrow, and I'll book your flight over as soon as I can get the ticket."

Things really are looking up!

Except, what the hell is wrong with my dog? He just recovered from the abscess. Could the infection have returned? I stick the cone of the thermometer in his ear, and he still registers a normal temperature. In fact, his temperature is actually a couple of degrees below normal. Maybe the stupid thermometer isn't working, or I didn't leave it in long enough. It beeped to signal that Chesty's temperature had been read, but I never really trust these things. Still, they beat the alternative method for taking a dog's temperature.

All night, I pet and stroke and worry over Chesty.

"Don't give up now," I tell him. "Dad found us a new house with a big yard for you. Maybe cats to chase."

"Cats" is a word that we spell around this dog. His response to hearing the dreaded C-word should be to catapult off the bed, race outside, and run frantically in circles with his nose to the ground looking for a fun feline chase. Tonight, I get no response at all. His eyes are definitely glassy now, his tongue hangs from the side of his mouth, and his breathing is shallow and erratic. Or else I'm imagining the whole thing and making my dog crazy with my emotional theatrics.

By morning, I decide to call the vet and get him over here. If he gets pissed and makes the trip for nothing, that's better than losing my dog because I waited too long to call. Watching Rocca gulp down her food and lap up water, it occurs to me that Chesty's bowl hasn't been touched. More worrisome, he hasn't had a drop to drink since yesterday morning—just before he discovered that little gray frog.

I call the veterinarian and jabber to him in broken Spanish. I eventually understand that he is telling me he cannot get to the island. No boats can cross in this storm. He tells me to be sure Chesty drinks plenty of water. I tell him the dog isn't drinking water or eating, and he tells me something that sounds ominous but which I don't understand. I do comprehend that he can't get here, and he'll call me when the weather clears and see if I still need him to come.

Looking up poison dart frogs of Bocas del Toro on the internet turns up the same pictures of the brightly colored tree frogs that I've seen on postcards for sale here in the grocery stores. The frog Chesty found in the yard was definitely gray. Dull gray. And I don't think the dog ever had the slimy little guy in his mouth. I suppose Chesty could have picked the frog up and had it in his mouth briefly before I got there, but still, that frog was gray, not red or bright yellow with red spots, which are common in this area. Just an ordinary little frog. His illness must be a relapse from the infection.

This morning, Chesty looks skeletal. He doesn't have any fat on him to begin with, and now, dehydrated, he looks nearly dead. I bring the water bowl to him, but he's not interested. Worse, he doesn't seem to register that it's there. I wonder if I could force water down his throat with a syringe? It doesn't seem likely.

Jack calls from the airport to say that he's there with the dog crate, but all flights to Bocas are canceled until the storm abates. He's going back to the hotel, and he'll call me from there. I've managed to get him worried about Chesty, too. He doesn't think forcing water down his throat is a good idea.

"He'll drink when he's thirsty. Maybe he knows how to take care of himself better than you do. Just keep him cool in the air conditioning. I'll try to get on the evening flight back."

Sally calls a few hours later. Apparently, Jack called her about Chesty. She tells me the storm is predicted to hang over us for another three or four days. Whatever is going to happen with my dog, it'll just be me here to help him. Neither Jack nor the vet can get to Bocas until the weather clears.

I mention the little gray frog to Sally and she says, "Oh, honey. Those little gray buggers are the most poisonous of all. They're the ones the Kuna Indians use for their blow darts."

I call the vet back and tell him about the frog. The only words I can make out are *morir* which means "die" and *probablemente* which needs no translation.

"Should I give the dog water?" I ask him in stumbling Spanish.

The vet's reply is a clear "No!" followed by a whole bunch of words that I don't catch at all. By the time I hang up, as near as I can figure, there's nothing I can do but to keep Chesty comfortable. Forcing him to take water is a bad idea. There is no antivenom for this frog poison. My dog is probably going to die no matter what I do.

After almost forty-eight hours of eating and drinking nothing and lying nearly motionless, Chesty raises his head shakily like someone coming off a really bad drunk. His eyes still don't seem to be seeing anything in this world, but when I offer him the water bowl, he manages to slurp up a few drops before dropping his head back onto the bed. Almost immediately, he vomits the water back up. This becomes our routine for the next three days. Each time he lifts his head, he drinks a tiny bit more water, and it seems to stay down for a little longer.

Jack, still stuck in the city, calls for updates on his dog. He's using the time to begin the process of getting a loan for the remainder of the money we'll need to purchase this wonderful house he's found. On Friday, after four days of howling winds and never-ending sheets of silver rain, the storm tires itself out, and we have blue sky over the islands. Jack is stranded in the city another day because the flights are backed up, but he's scheduled to be back in Bocas tomorrow.

This morning, for the first time, Chesty keeps water down. When he's up and staggering a few hours later, I leave him to run to the local market and return with rice and hamburger to see if I can tempt him to eat. He follows me down the stairs and watches me cook his food, but he won't touch it when I put it in front of him. Rocca, however, is ecstatic to be having her favorite food in the world. Much better than those old kibbles we usually make her eat.

The band has returned but is diminished. Either the kids have grown tired of the game or most of the instruments didn't survive their mothers' wrath during the storm-enforced house arrest. Either way, the musicians have thinned to a dissolute little group who half-heartedly drag tin cans behind them on soggy twine. The hubcap cymbals, thank God, seem to have disappeared. I watch the kids regroup and the guys at the taxi depot busily wash pickup taxis. From the corner of my eye, I see the little rock thrower in the torn tank top rear back to hurl a fifty-cent piece-sized rock at Chesty, who's swaying on his feet with his tail going in wavy half-circles.

If the local population ever rises up against the *gringos* who've encroached on their land and slaughter them in their sleep before disappearing into the green jungle with machetes dripping the blood of the invaders, this little guy will be the rebel leader—it will be a delayed reaction to being terrorized by the crazy white woman who lived next to him briefly when he was no more than a helpless toddler. Upon seeing the little monster with his arm behind him, ready to hurl this missile at Chesty, I become a raving lunatic.

I materialize at the fence, scream obscenities, and threaten to tear the child limb from limb and feed him, bloody piece by piece, to my dogs. Since this is all in English, the child can only interpret my tone. Hopefully. I stoop and pick up a handful of rocks which I then actually throw at the child. I miss, but not for lack of trying. The child's face morphs from mischievous to terror-stricken. He stands his ground for a few seconds, then drops his rock and flees into his house from where I'm sure his mother will be coming to decapitate me for threatening her baby boy.

I'm still screaming when I notice the guys across the street at the taxi depot laughing and giving me the thumbs-up sign. Hopefully this has the same meaning here as it does back home. Damien the rock hurler's mother hasn't shown up, and one of the English-speaking mechanics from across the street wanders over just before the dogs and I retreat upstairs.

"That boy, he is a problem," he tells me with a grin.

I've had enough time now to feel badly about my behavior, and I tell him, "I'm sorry. I shouldn't have thrown rocks at him."

"No, no!" He laughs. "We all throw the rocks at this one. Is no problem."

So, I still feel guilty, but at least the child's mother probably isn't going to be coming for me with a machete.

By Friday evening, Chesty has eaten a little and he is holding down water. He no longer looks dead. The vet calls to check on him and to see if, now that the storm is over, I need him to make the crossing. I tell him about the little progress Chesty has made. He says he will not come to the island then. At least, I think that's what he says.

Sally calls right after and tells me that Camelia spoke with the vet too. Apparently, he told her he has never known a dog to survive an encounter with a poison dart frog. He thinks Chesty's size and the fact that he probably only sniffed at the frog and didn't actually have the amphibian in his mouth saved his life. He told Camelia that most of the dog's hallucinations should be over now and suggested I keep an eye on him and encourage him to drink water and eat what he can.

The good news is that, with his hallucinating and all, Chesty has missed the first two days of Rocca's heat cycle, and he's still way too weak to hold himself up on two legs while he jumps her. We might actually be safe until Jack arrives with the crate. Rocca behaves exactly like her human counterpart would if her man abandoned her at her sexual peak to go off on some hallucinogenic trip. She tries the human equivalent of batting her eyelashes and flirting coyly, meaning she wafts her butt near his nose and then turns to lick his face and whimper doggy encouragement. When this fails to get her the attention she wants, she goes from coy to aggressive, pushing the part of her body that needs his attention against him and backing up. In doing this, she manages to push him down the entire flight of stairs. This does nothing to increase his stamina or desire for her big, hot body.

Rocca makes a last-ditch effort for his attention. In the yard, she waves her big ass at every male dog that comes down the fence line. Several of the mangy neighborhood bad boys are interested, but none is willing to get close enough to get a good sniff. Chesty reminds me of that rich, old, near-dead guy that married Anna Nicole Smith. He lies on the downstairs patio where he landed after his tumble down the stairs. Each time a young stud appears, he raises his head and growls menacingly. Like the old billionaire, his message is clear.

"You're right, Bucko, she's hot, but she's all mine, and you don't even want to think about crossing me to get to her. Move on and find yourself a girl more suitable to your station in life."

This message is delivered low and rumbling and followed by an ear-ringing bark that communicates clearly, "*NOW, ASSHOLE!*"

Rocca's fan club backs off and watches from the shade of a palm tree on the corner. I can see them discussing the situation among themselves.

"Oh yeah, he thinks he's tough, but he's gotta fall asleep sometime."

"You said it, Slim. That bitch is hot for my body. Did you see the look she gave me?"

"I'd like to see that big muther come over here and talk that shit to us."

"We'd tear him to pieces!"

"We'd clean the street with his ass!"

"Oh shit! Is he up and walking now?"

"You don't think he can get out of that fence, do ya?"

"Naw. No way."

"Well. That's lucky for him 'cause we'd kick his pedigreed ass!"

I bring both dogs upstairs. Chesty doesn't need the aggravation, and it's not unheard of for dogs to successfully breed through cyclone fences—

though these neighborhood dogs would have to balance on each other's backs to reach Rocca. Still, I bring her in, and my dogs arrange themselves again on the plastic-backed bedspread we've packed all the way from Arizona. Chesty's breathing is now even and deep. Rocca curls up with her butt against his face, then sighs in obvious disgust and resignation, giving up. Soon, she drifts off to, no doubt, some doggy fantasy that is best left to the imagination.

TWENTY-ONE
AN ADJUSTMENT OF EXPECTATIONS

I T'S MY TURN to fly to Panama City and meet with the realtors. I'm excited about seeing the house we're in the process of buying, but I'm even more enthusiastic about getting a hot shower. I know it sounds like a refreshing idea, in the tropics, to shower in cold water. The reality is not as swell as you might think.

Our bathroom in Bocas has no windows and is always the coolest spot in the house. We've just come out of a six-day storm that dropped temperatures from the low 90s to the very cold 60s. Hey! I see you up there in Idaho or Wisconsin or wherever the hell you are, rolling your eyes and shaking your hardy pioneer-stock shoulders in disgust. Screw you and the oxen you rode in on! I admit it. I'm temperature challenged.

Even when it's 90 degrees, a cold-water shower isn't all that wonderful. It does cool me off if I just do one of those quick rinses I call a bird bath and Jack, in his much more colorful way, calls a whore's bath. But if I take a real, honest-to-God shower, by the time I spend ten minutes under cold water wetting, washing, and rinsing my hair, I'm shivering. Cold showers actually increase body temperature anyway, making it that much more unpleasant when I step out into the humidity and heat of the rest of the house.

Poor me. Just go on outside and shovel some snow or scrape the icicles off the roof or whatever it is you do up north for fun in the dark of the long desolate winters. Warm yourself with your feelings of superiority over this pampered, spoiled *gringo* living in the tropics. Go ahead. I give you my personal permission to gloat a little as you slip and slide on the ice and pray this isn't the day you're going to fall and break a hip, starting that inexorable slide into inevitable death. Me? I'm on a flight to Panama City where, once checked into my room at the Las Vegas Suites, I intend to enjoy about an hour under a shower hot enough to cook vegetables.

Jack has warned me that the Veneto Casino—which, you remember, is catty-corner from the hotel—has now added a new noisemaker to its repertoire. This device sounds as though WWIII has broken out. Evidently, the casino broadcasts this mimic of an atomic blast, complete with everything but the mushroom cloud, whenever anyone in the casino wins over ten dollars. They still shoot off the mortar attack mimics for the two-dollar winners. This newer, bigger, better sound effect is an extra, added attraction. Jack spent much of his last stay at the hotel diving for cover or low-crawling to a protective wall. Suffice it to say, his PTSD wasn't improved by this experience.

I've never been in a war zone, but two minutes after checking into the hotel, I'm ready to massacre whoever is responsible for this outrage of sound. It is pointed out to me, however, by the unfortunate folks who work at the hotel and must endure this noise twelve hours a day, six days a week, that the owner of the casino is a politically-connected drug lord. Feeling like one of Rocca's would-be suitors, I retreat to my room and mumble that I'd better not catch the bastard outside without his body guards.

By the following day, just before noon, Leo, Annabella, and I are in San Carlos. We cruise the village and the beach before the young realtors show me the property Jack and I are buying. San Carlos is a tiny place with hundreds of houses that seem vacant. Annabella explains that almost everyone who owns a home here only lives in them a few weekends a year. The rest of the time the houses are maintained and guarded by live-in servants. We drive along the clean, attractive streets, and I look out the passenger window at one beautiful home after another. It begins to sink in how much money there is in this country.

"So, these are Panamanians who own these houses?" I ask.

"Most of them, yes. Some *gringos* are discovering and moving to the area. San Carlos is only ten minutes from Coronado, which was the first gated community on this coast. Coronado now has lots of *gringos*."

"Huh. That's a lot of money to maintain a home in the city and then another here at the beach. Especially when you only come here a few weeks a year."

"Yes," Leo tells me, "most families in Panama have several country houses."

"Several?"

"Usually one retreat in a Pacific coast beach town, a couple more in the many mountain towns near here, one in Bocas del Toro, and another on the Pearl Islands."

"That's a lot of money!" I exclaim as I watch a gardener trimming the hibiscus hedge of a large lime-green house with a swimming pool.

"The houses are owned jointly by all the family members. So it doesn't take as much money as you might think. A family of 125 people—cousins and aunties and uncles and whatnot—they might own, between them, two dozen houses. These houses have been in the same family, passed down from generation to generation, for years. The family shares in the maintenance, and they build on over the years. It's a good system."

"So, how much does it cost to have a full-time couple to do all the maintenance and cooking and cleaning?"

"A couple? Maid and gardener? About two hundred dollars a month."

"Really? And where do these people live? The ones who are the servants in these houses?"

"In the servants' quarters of the big houses mostly. But they usually also have family houses back further in the jungle outside of town."

"Huh. So, the house we're getting. The gardener there makes how much a month?"

"He's making one hundred twenty dollars, but that's because the house sits on two full hectares. About five acres. And also because he's been working there since he was fifteen. So, he's a good worker and knows how to take care of the house. I think the couple that you're buying the house from are very fond of him and choose to pay him a little more than the going rate. You can pay him whatever you agree on with him."

As we cross the highway and make our way down a paved road, past a beautiful river with overhanging trees, this place begins to remind me a little of the Old South. Before the War of Northern Aggression mucked it up for those lucky few pampered plantation owners. Could I get used to letting someone else do all the work for me? I actually think maybe I could, yeah.

The house we pull up in front of looks like a small bed and breakfast set in a park. This is my new home. I am stunned. Before I'm even out of the car, I know the rest of the visit is only perfunctory. I love this house. A part of my brain is doing its best to whisper that the house certainly has what realtors call "curb appeal," but that doesn't mean it's actually going to measure up to our needs. I pay almost no attention to this voice. I've always been a sucker for a pretty face. By the time I've been given the grand tour and met José, the gardener, my critical little voice is silent.

I do my best to wipe the silly grin off my face as the older gentleman who is selling the house leads our little group around from room to room. He might still try and raise the price. I try to look dismayed at the tiny kitchen or shocked at the lack of hot water at the kitchen sink. I fail miserably. I like small kitchens, and we can put in a demand hot water heater for under fifty dollars. The master bath has hot water. That pretty much seals the deal for me.

I follow the seller as he points out dozens of tablecloths, dishes, and glassware to serve one hundred, plus a set of silver for twenty with four spoons missing. More kitchen gadgets and towels and sheets and even a hair dryer all come with the house. There's even a brand-new riding lawn mower and a working 1951 Willys Army Jeep. I walk the fence line before we leave and satisfy myself that my dogs won't be able to get out anywhere along its length.

Annabella walks with me. She explains that the old gentleman is married to the sister of a former Panamanian president. They are a very honorable, old Panamanian family. These kinds of houses rarely come up for sale as the families hold on to them at all costs. But this particular house is owned exclusively by this old couple. No brothers or sisters or cousins are involved.

The couple bought the land and originally built the house as a place for the husband to put his horse. He is an old Colombian Cavalry officer, and when he retired, he took his horse and his Jeep with him. They are selling because they're too old to make the trip from their apartment in the city much anymore, and because they have a son who is in need of cancer treatment and they need the cash money to pay the doctors.

I call Jack as we're leaving the house.

"You know how we always buy a place, get all enthusiastic about it, and then get bored and sell it five years later? Well, this time I think we'd better go ahead and reserve a place for ourselves in the San Carlos cemetery. If we can get into this place, I ain't leavin' until they carry me out feet first."

Back on Bocas, Jack has been busy in my absence. Both of us are energized now that we've found the house of our dreams. Well, the house of our modified dreams. We're aware that this isn't the lifestyle we chased down here. We thought we were going to live on a little jungle island in the blue Caribbean Sea. Enjoy a simple life in a small rustic house with just a few comforts. This Pacific coast house seems a little like the life my mom would enjoy rather than something I would choose.

The reality is that, as we get older, this balancing act with comfort and adventure—the two weights on opposite ends of our desire—is being adjusted. We get progressively closer along the bar to comfort as its weight increases in importance to us. Instead of a tree house in the jungle, we're going to live in a plantation-style bed and breakfast that we have all to ourselves.

It's an adjustment in expectation for us, but I think we're going to do just fine. Jack is back to singing the old Beatles song, "Here Comes the Sun." I haven't collapsed in a heap of tears for days. Rocca is just about over her latest heat cycle, and Chesty is recovered from his misadventures and is once again his normal, frisky self.

Now we just have to figure out how to get ourselves off this island in the Caribbean and back to the Pacific coast. This is a little more difficult than we imagined. We can't hire a taxi from the island. We could take a boat and arrive in Almirante, the armpit of the country, with our dogs and luggage and hope to hire a taxi from there. This would leave us in a position of enormous disadvantage while we negotiate with the driver. The feeling here among the *gringos* we consult is that we'd end up paying two arms and probably a leg. A fair price would be a couple hundred dollars. What we'd probably pay is almost certainly closer to $1,000.

Okay. So we'll fly out. Except there are a couple of challenges to that path too. There's only one flight a week off Bocas on a commercial plane with a cargo hold big enough for a dog crate large enough for one of the dogs. That flight leaves each Wednesday. No matter what we offer to pay, no one will allow us to fly commercial with the dogs in the passenger section. This is understandable as these are small planes. Even Jack can't figure out where dogs this size would fit. One of us would have to fly out with one dog on a Wednesday. The other would have to wait on the island with the other dog until the middle of the following week. This is possible. We just don't want to do it.

In the best of times, as I'm sure you've gathered by now, we are not known for making decisions based on reason and patience. Right now, we are both as frantic to get off these islands as we were to get on them a little less than two months ago. Jack makes arrangements to hire a single engine plane and pilot to carry him and the dogs to Panama City. I will follow the same day with all the luggage on a commercial airplane.

"Single engine?" I ask when my husband tells me this plan. "Wouldn't a twin engine plane be better?"

"Nothing's going to happen to the engine," he tells me in his Rocca's-not-going-to-jump-out-that-window great-and-powerful-Oz voice.

"Does the pilot understand that he's going to be flying you *and* two giant, uncrated dogs?"

"No problem. He met Chesty and knows Rocca's a little bigger. He says as long as the dogs don't move around during the flight, we'll be fine."

"What? Don't move around? You mean like leap up if a bird flies by or if they get into a disagreement while they're crammed together?"

"They'll be fine. The pilot will take out the back seat to make room for the dogs. One of them will have enough room to lie down, and the other can stand and look out the window."

"So Rocca will be lying down, and Chesty will be peering around politely?"

"Exactly."

I hate this arrangement, but I can't think of a better one. Jack wouldn't listen to me even if I could come up with a plan less likely to instigate the crash of a small plane into the triple canopy jungle. My husband is jazzed about flying out with both dogs on a tiny plane. It is going to provide his adrenaline rush for the month. I pray and hope for the best.

We have contacted the landlords of the yellow house here on Bocas. We paid them three months' rent in advance and are now leaving after only forty-six days. They are relieved that we're vacating the house. It turns out that their family has been angry with them for renting the house during the Christmas season. Apparently, they have always come over for a two-week party at the beach. The soonest they can get here from the mainland to return the rest of our money is the morning we leave, so I assume we can kiss that $1,200 goodbye. We chalk it up as one more very expensive consequence of coming to these islands.

We also paid a $150 deposit for the little internet antenna we've been using. I have been certain all along we'd never get this money back, but at the time we agreed to it, I was so desperate to communicate with people back home that access to the internet was the equivalent of medication. We bitched, but we paid it.

We walk uptown with the dogs and leave a message for the owner of the internet provider stating that we're leaving and that he needs to come and remove his equipment and return our deposit. Jack assures the clerk he will take the equipment with him if we don't get our money back. Of course, Jack also insists that the landlord will be arriving at the crack of dawn on the morning we're scheduled to leave to return our $1,200. I don't care anymore. I just pray to get off the island missing nothing more than my hacked off arm.

We take Sally out to dinner as thanks for all she's done for us. It's fun to play tourist and blow a little money in one of the beautiful restaurants along the bay. She asked to see some of the pictures we have on our laptop from our trip to Asia, so we bring the computer with us and do a slide show as she and Jack sip pineapple daiquiris and I work on my Diet Coke with ice.

The ice is a glorious luxury, and I enjoy every shivery, cold sip. Dinner is wonderful, and afterward we say goodbye and walk back home under a sky streaked with stars between wide bands of clouds.

At home, we discover that we've forgotten the computer at the restaurant. I stay with the dogs, and Jack rushes back uptown. All our personal information is on the laptop, including our bank accounts and passwords. By the time Jack returns, his little daiquiri buzz is long gone, but he has the computer in hand. The waitress tucked it behind the bar and was on the phone with Sally, telling her it had been left, when Jack walked in to claim it. It's very confusing when, just when you decide a culture is so different from your own that you simply cannot live within its confines, you're kissed on the lips by the general honesty and goodness of its people.

The following day, with one night left before our scheduled departure, the internet guy shows up, removes his equipment, and returns all of our deposit. Wow! Now, if the landlord shows up with our prepaid rent, we'll be batting a thousand. We've hired Diego, the older brother of the little rock-throwing monster-child, to clean house for us. He's been coming once a week. We don't really need him, but giving him the job created goodwill with the little pukes in the band. He comes on our last day and scrubs the floors and walls and leaves the house cleaner than we found it a month and a half ago. We send him home with his measly pay, along with all the foodstuffs in the cupboards.

The next morning, just before dawn, we're up and ready to go. We wait until the last minute to walk to the airport as the landlord hasn't yet arrived. The neighborhood kids troop over to stand in front of our place and wave goodbye. They almost make me sorry I've had such nasty thoughts about them. We hoped for a taxi but can't find one this early, so we head on out with the dogs on leashes, dragging our luggage behind us. Three of the older boys, about eight years old, rush forward when they see us and take the suitcases from us, wide grins on their faces. This is going to end up costing us more than if we'd taken a taxi, but we don't care. It's a much nicer way to leave the island. Now if the landlord will just show up!

At the airport, we say our final goodbyes to the neighbor kids, pass out money, and go inside the terminal. I check our luggage onto my commercial flight, and Jack checks in with his pilot. My husband comes back to say that his plane is ready to go and cleared for takeoff, so he's going to load the dogs and get out of here. If the landlord shows up, I'll take the money. If not, we'll deal with it from Panama City. In the lavender-tinged light of early morning, I walk Jack to his plane and see it for the first time.

It looks like something a person would hang below to throw themselves off a cliff. There is no way Jack and both dogs are going to fit inside the coffin-sized passenger section of this plane. Except they do. The dogs have just enough room to wedge themselves behind the two seats. As predicted, Rocca lies down almost immediately. Chesty stands, turning his head from one porthole window to the other or gazing forward as though studying the instrument panel, his nose about eighteen inches away from the controls.

Watching everything I have in the world disappear inside that plane as the pilot forces the passenger door closed, I peer down and check the underside of the plane.

"What ya looking for?" the pilot asks.

"Pontoons," I say. "I thought there'd be pontoons since most of the flight is over water."

"*Over* water," says the pilot, who seems perfectly sane and responsible as long as you don't consider that he just locked two humongous, uncrated dogs into his tiny plane. "Not *in* the water." He winks at me. "I'll get them to Panama City safely. No worries."

Then they're gone, and I'm left standing on the tarmac alone watching this toy plane waddle down the runway and slip up into the air.

Back inside the terminal, the landlord is waiting for me with a wad of money in his hand. Jesus God, we may get off this island in one piece yet.

TWENTY-TWO
CHESTY LEARNS TO FLY
AND ROCCA GOES ALONG FOR THE RIDE

A DOG-LESS FLIGHT over deep-blue water, sprinkled with vibrant islets trimmed in snowy white sand carries me toward the Tocumen International Airport in Panama City. I enjoy every responsibility-free minute of it. A little animal in my head insists on conjuring images of a tiny plane falling into the turquoise sea, but I lecture my wild tag-along that there is nothing I can do about that possibility. The pointy-nosed beast finally shuts up and disappears back into the depth of my head where it's no doubt feeding on my doubts and fears and growing sleek and fat. I choose to ignore the gnawing critter, have another mango juice, and enjoy the ride.

When the commercial flight lands in Panama City, I collect my bags and head to the front of the airport to wait for my family to drop from the sky and join me. Halfway across the tiny terminal, I notice a crowd of people rushing for the windows that look out on the landing strip. That internal voice leaps to the front of my head and sinks his fangs into my fear where it conjures a vision of a tiny, bent and broken plane crashed on the runway. I maneuver my luggage to the window where I can see what the excitement is all about. Jack is strolling across the tarmac, Chesty heeling on his right side, Rocca on his left. Two properly-caped and perfectly-behaved service dogs at work.

Airport security has a cocker spaniel working as a drug-sniffer. This little dog takes one look at these two intruders from what is clearly another reality entirely, yelps, tucks its docked tail between its legs, and drags its trainer to the safety of a nearby glassed-in room. Cockers are small but bright. The crowd cheers and claps and laughs. Jack grins like visiting royalty, Chesty steps up his strut, and Rocca, ever-vigilant on the job, swings her big head from side to side, watching for any danger. I am simply relieved to see the worry-rodent lying dead as a door nail, ugly pink feet straight in the air. Hopefully this time he really is dead and not just "playing possum."

While I'm greeting Jack and the dogs, luggage handlers appear as if from thin air. They vie for the job of taking our bags the four steps remaining to the front of the airport. From there, we will try to find a taxi to take us and the dogs to our home away from home, the Las Vegas Suites, where we will wait for the deal to finalize so we can move into our new house.

Jack's booming laugh echoes in the terminal. He chats to the crowd in broken Spanish while a few brave individuals edge forward to sneak a hand down and touch one of the dogs. I play my usual role as spoil sport, and seeing how he is handling both leashes, I take control of Rocca and beg Jack, as a personal favor to me, to actually hold Chesty's leash in his hand and not just drape it over his shoulder with the loop end hanging at his waist. He gives me a heavy sigh of disappointment, but he holds the leash.

Jack chooses a black Nissan X-Trail with side windows tinted so heavily that peons along the road will be unable to see us as we are whisked along the city streets to our next temporary abode. The chosen luggage handler loads the bags and collects his generous tip. Jack climbs into the front seat, and Chesty leaps flat-footed from the ground to his lap in one jump.

"Ha! Ha! Ha!" laughs Jack.

The driver, who has reduced his fare for the entertainment value of retelling the story of these crazy *gringos* and their massive dogs, laughs less heartily. The other taxi drivers, who were aced out when Jack chose this vehicle, laugh loudest of all.

I climb in the back seat, and Rocca, after one final look over her shoulder at the crowd, follows me inside, less athletically than Chesty, but looking much more regal. I can see the other taxi drivers slapping each other on the back and laughing it up big time as we pull away.

"A little different from our taxi rides on Bocas, huh?"

Jack grins at me in the rearview mirror.

On Bocas del Toro, taxis just keep picking up new riders. They drop passengers off as they come to their stop and pick up more as they make slow progress toward their final destination. In the last cab we were in on Bocas, Jack was in the front passenger seat holding an old Kuna woman, who wore the traditional beaded leg wrappings and silver nose rings, on his lap. On grandma's lap was a little boy about two years old. Jack, of course, spent the ride making that popping noise with his finger in the side of his mouth, much to the delight of the little guy and trepidation of the grandma. I was in the backseat under a young woman with a laundry bag of clothes on her lap. Beside me was a man holding his wife on his lap, and next to him was a teenage boy holding a plastic bag of groceries and his mother. The taxi was an eight-year-old, two-door Toyota sedan.

I've got a nice bruise from the broken armrest in the Bocas Toyota that's now turning that promising yellow, which means in another week or two it'll be gone. So yeah, this Nissan with the mafia windows is a nice change of pace for us.

"So," I ask, now that we're out of the crowd, "how did the dogs do on the flight?"

"The pilot said they were the best passengers he's had in a long time! Rocca lifted her head to look out the window every once in a while and just relaxed the rest of the time. Chesty got a little nervous when we went through that rain squall. When the plane rocked and rolled a little and disappeared in the cloud bank, he pushed his head between me and the pilot, then studied the instrument panel like he was wondering if he could fly the thing if he had to."

"Oh!" I remember to tell him, "The landlord showed up just as you took off. He gave me back all the money."

"See, I told you everything would work out okay."

I have a tiny urge to beat my wonderful, happy husband over the head with, oh I don't know, a dead possum. But I smile at him instead. Really, he's hard to resist when he's on a roll.

We move back into the Las Vegas Suites on the fifth of December. This time around, management has decreed that we pay twenty dollars a day more for the room because of the dogs. They claim, no doubt rightfully, that the entire room had to be wiped down and everything had to be laundered, including the bedspreads and drapes, after our last stay. Since they pay their cleaning staff six dollars a day, we find it hard to believe that it actually cost them all that much to clean the room, but we're stuck between a rock and a hard place. We agree to pay them seventy-eight dollars a day for the room.

The increase in price takes some of the wind out of Jack's sails, but after a nice hot shower and a meal down the street at our old haunt, Molina's, he's back in good cheer again—temporarily. Unfortunately, the casino is still doing its air strike imitation every few minutes and detonating its imitation atom bomb approximately each half hour. This, coupled with the increase in the price of the room, sends Jack on a phone search for another hotel. Three hours later, he's spoken with every manager at every hotel in the Panama City phone book. None of them will take the dogs. So, it looks like this is home sweet home for the moment.

Right about now is when Jack's PTSD begins to kick into overdrive. As I mentioned, this time of year is always difficult for him because of combat anniversary dates. Living with a dozen or so simulated mortar attacks each hour seems to be exacerbating his symptoms rather significantly. Paying twenty dollars a night more than he expected for the hotel room isn't helping his cheap soul either.

Leo calls to say the bank has approved our loan on the house. However, there are a few glitches. Banks in Panama will not loan money to anyone over seventy years old. Since Jack is sixty, the term on the loan can't be more than ten years. This is no problem, we want a seven-year loan. The second, teeny challenge is that banks require a life insurance policy for the amount of the loan, so Jack needs to go for a physical. He and Leo are set up with the insurance company doctor two days from now.

To me, the interesting part of this legal requirement is that the insurance policy is not a decreasing term. Jack must get a standard life insurance policy for the full amount of the original loan. As the loan is paid down, we will still be paying the full premium and have the original coverage. Supposedly, if Jack died, the insurance would pay off the loan and I would receive the remainder of the money. If approved, the policy is going to add $138 a month to our loan payment.

As it turns out, this is the least of our problems. Four days of simulated mortar attacks and atomic blasts, blaring car horns, and congested traffic later, the insurance company turns Jack down for the life insurance policy because his EKG shows a past heart attack. The EKG is telling the truth. His heart did stop at one point, but it wasn't because of a heart attack. His heart stopped when he died in Vietnam after stepping on the land mine. That was thirty-five years ago, and he's had no heart problems since then. This, however, turns out to be an explanation that doesn't translate well. The doctor won't clear Jack for the coverage.

"No problem," says Leo. "We will find another life insurance company that will approve you. By the way, the home owners haven't cleared the house through the utility companies yet or provided an appraisal. But, no problem, these are honorable people. No need to worry."

The next explosion from the casino next door sends Jack flat to the floor. Evidently, there is a direct correlation between controlling his environment and dealing with stress-inducers. Exactly like they tell you in all those psychology books about PTSD. We take the dogs for a walk to get the hell out of the room for a while. Caught in the afternoon rain storm, we duck into an outdoor restaurant and load up on rich, fatty, grease-fried food to comfort ourselves and make all our problems go away.

It doesn't work all that well. Nonetheless, we don't give up hope on this coping strategy. Over the next week, Jack is turned down by three more insurance companies, and the owners of the house still haven't provided the papers necessary to complete the sale. Even though Leo and Annabella assure us that the family from whom we are desperately trying to buy the house are honorable and honest people, we get our own attorney. We have been told over and over by *gringos* and Panamanians alike that this is necessary down here.

There are no title companies in Panama. The banks and realtors together handle the sale. Since both these entities have a vested interest in the deal going through, this seems to us a bad idea. Which is why we hire our own attorney, Jorge Kosmos. Mr. Kosmos is a Greek-Panamanian—another example of the cosmopolitan complexion of this country. He advises us to form a corporation. This is a legal way to get out of paying taxes when we sell the house. If and when that time comes, we will simply sell the corporation, a transaction which is not taxed. He also starts the paperwork to split the property into four sections. This will make it easier to sell in the future, but more importantly, Panama does not tax unimproved property, so it will save us paying yearly taxes on the full two hectares of land.

Clever, these attorneys.

All this work with Mr. Kosmos is an investment into a deal that looks, increasingly, as though it may not go through. Leo and Annabella are doing their best to support and nurture us like the clueless babes in the woods that we are down here. We are doing our best to go along with the program and not worry. This isn't working all that well. Not to mention, the casino has now begun to set off fireworks and, more disturbingly, fire crackers, from nine to midnight each night.

Jack's starting to get angry.

We don't want an angry Jack. He very rarely allows himself to experience the full depth of this emotion. Mostly because he slides very quickly from anger to rage. He's never really gotten past that fight-or-flight reflex he learned so well on his first jungle adventure. So we wait, though not at all patiently.

During my last pregnancy, my son stayed inside three weeks past his due date. By the time he was born, I had decided I was going to be pregnant forever. A rare phenomenon, but nonetheless what was happening, of that I had been sure. I feel the same way now. The Las Vegas Suites is our Hotel California. We can check in, but we can never leave.

Realtors and bankers assure us the deal is going through and we will be in our new house by next week. I'm convinced they're all wrong. We're never going to leave this hotel. We'll just live here, among the mortar rounds and atomic explosions, riding up and down in the glass elevator with Chesty peering out at the restaurant diners and Rocca flattened against the floor, until all our money is gone and we weigh six hundred pounds from the

Dunkin' Donuts and the Baskin-Robbins' double-dish-fudge sundaes from across the street. It's our fate. There's no way to fight against it. Better to just give in and have another doughnut.

While I sink further into lethargy, Jack calls the bank, the realtors, and the owners and explains that he is a very impatient and unhappy *gringo*. He will be taking his money and his dogs and leaving on the first of January if the deal isn't finalized and he isn't in his new house by New Year's Eve. Leo arrives to take us to dinner where he explains that this is not the United States. This is Panama. Latin America. Things don't work here the way they work up north. There is no problem with the deal on the house. No worries. Everything will be good. We must just be patient a little longer.

Jack explains that he cannot do this. His patience is gone. Money is running through his fingers each day we stay at the hotel. First of January, at 9:47 p.m. we have plane tickets back to the States and we're leaving.

In fact, we do have tickets to fly out on January 1st. Round trip tickets are cheaper to buy than one way, and that's the arbitrary date we gave for our scheduled return flight. However, I cannot go through this whole procedure again, in another hotel room in the States, while we start from scratch to find a house to buy there. I beg Jack not to follow through on this threat.

He's not listening. He's done.

The bank, the sellers, the realtors—they have two and a half weeks to put this deal together. The first of January, we're either in the house in San Carlos, or we're out of here and starting over someplace else.

During the next week, Leo finds a company that insures Jack for the amount of the bank loan. The day before Christmas, our attorney receives everything he needs from the sellers. Now, we wait on the bank to do the final paperwork so we can sign and move into the house. On December 30th, we haven't signed anything, and Jack is packing to return to the States while I frantically try to convince him that we're better off waiting just a little longer here than starting over somewhere else.

Leo calls the next morning to say he's picking Jack up at ten to go to the bank and sign the papers. We can move into the San Carlos house tonight, New Year's Eve. At noon, Leo still hasn't arrived at the hotel. Jack is in that

CLUELESS GRINGOS IN PARADISE 171

state of fury that looks like near-comatose calm if you overlook his shaking hands and the bright, crazed look in his eyes. I am experiencing my very own near-death experience.

Leo appears at 4:00 p.m. to take Jack to the bank to sign the papers. Jack brings Chesty in the hope his trusty service dog will help to keep him from strangling someone in the event that the deal doesn't happen. The attorney and the sellers are to meet Leo and Jack at the bank. I know I do something between four and seven, when Jack returns, but I have no recollection of what it is. I think I just lie on the bed, bathed in the white light of acceptance and cease to exist.

I can hear Jack as he steps from the elevator. In his deep baritone, he belts out, "Swing low, sweet chariot. Coming for to carry me home!"

The bedside clock says 7:14 p.m. Are we going to the airport or to our new home in San Carlos? When Jack and Chesty step in the room and I see my husband's sparkling eyes, I know we're staying in Panama.

"Madam," he greets me. "Your chariot awaits."

"We got the house?"

"Of course. Was there ever any doubt? The taxi's waiting downstairs to take us to our new home."

TWENTY-THREE
HOME SWEET HOME

THE TWO-HOUR taxi ride from the city to San Carlos is interesting. Even at almost nine at night, the city is one big traffic jam. It's New Year's Eve, and judging by the number of vehicles that weave and swerve their way along the medians and sidewalks, the celebrations have started early.

Our taxi driver has been working since four this morning, running a group of visiting German fishermen across the isthmus, stopping at several rivers and lakes in between the two oceans. He falls asleep no less than fifteen times before we pull into San Carlos. The last time, Jack actually has to reach over and shake him to get him to wake up before we plunge off the road.

Arriving in San Carlos, we have another little challenge. We've only seen the house once. Where exactly is it again? Thankfully, it's not that difficult to locate, and we pull into the drive just before midnight after only a few wrong turns. Once we find the correct street, we see all the outdoor lights are on and the gardener, José, is standing in the driveway waiting to open the gate for us. I think I may be dreaming all this, but I'm going to enjoy the feeling of relief while I can—dream, hallucination, whatever it may be.

Once the driver has been paid, with recommendations from both Jack and me to pull over and get some sleep before heading back to the city, we turn the dogs loose on the lush, rolling green grass of their new five-acre yard. Rocca sniffs and explores carefully, but Chesty simply runs flat out at top speed from one end of the five acres to the other. Then he runs the perimeter, leaning into the four corner turns. He comes to a dead stop then, as though an idea has just occurred to him, and throws himself on the lush, green grass where he rolls and kicks his feet in the air and squirms, twisting his back from side-to-side. He jumps up after a few minutes of this and races around the yard some more, stops, throws himself down, and rolls again.

While this is going on, José has brought in our luggage and managed to communicate a question about when we want him to unpack for us. We send him off to bed in his quarters on the property while we return to watching the dogs enjoy their freedom. At midnight, we learn that people in San Carlos love pyrotechnics just as much as that guy who owns the casino in the city.

This time though, the fireworks sound less like mortar rounds and more like a welcome to our new home. Standing side by side, our arms around each other's waists, we watch the fireworks in the village below us. It's hard to believe that we actually survived this ordeal of moving to Panama with our two giant dogs. Like the hiker in Utah probably felt, I still suspect I'm going to wake at any moment to discover I'm held fast in the insurmountable mess into which I so naively plunged myself.

EPILOGUE
COME ON DOWN

WE'VE BEEN LIVING happily in our new home for almost two years now. Things have turned out both better and harder than we expected they would. I thought it would take a while to become accustomed to having someone else do all the work in my house. Wrong. By the second or third day, I was lifting my feet so José could sweep and mop under them. I bought plants at one of the many nurseries, and after bringing them home, discovered that "*Señora*" was expected to tell José where to plant her purchases, not get her own hands dirty doing the work of putting them in the ground. I've always enjoyed the feel of dirt between my fingers, so it took me a full five minutes to get into the swing of this new system.

We learned to never mention in José's earshot that we might want anything that is within his power to provide. When Jack complained that our grapefruit trees where no longer producing, José arrived the next morning with a basket of grapefruit from someone else's tree. When I strolled out to one of our lime trees to pluck a few limes to season the fish we were having for dinner, José raced across the yard to pick them for me and gave me the now-familiar look which I, from early on, understood to mean, "*Señora* is to tell me what she wants, and I will get it for her." Okay. Can do.

The more we discovered about the house, the luckier we felt. After meeting a few of our neighbors, we decided to throw a small *fiesta*. José asked what we were serving. He then retrieved from cupboards I didn't even know we had, a serving dish specific for each appetizer, entrée, and dessert. Fish-shaped platters. Dishes decorated with dancing chickens. My personal favorite is the one with the pigs chasing each other around the platter trying to stick meat thermometers into each other's hindquarters. That one is big enough on which to serve the whole porker. The selection of glasses—wine, champagne, aperitif, highball, and beer—made it nearly a requirement to serve a rich variety of beverages.

Once I got over feeling as though we were the only guests at a bed and breakfast where the owners were missing, I grew to love the house more and more. I also discovered that San Carlos is a wonderful location. In the dry season, I walk to the river in the afternoons to cool off at a swimming hole that looks like something out of a travel magazine. Huge flowering trees overhang the clear water where small fish swim in the shallows. Pairs of blue-crowned motmots and flocks of parrots scold me for interrupting their afternoon *siestas* as I plunge into water that is just cool enough to refresh me in the heat of the day. Floating on my back, looking up at the patterns the trees etch in the sunlight, I usually manage to frighten myself at least once each afternoon when, for a split second, my mind conjures up an alligator or venomous snake, and I nearly drown myself before sheepishly picking the dead leaf or twig off my arm and going on with my swim.

The ocean is a twenty-minute walk from the house, and I stroll the beach a couple of times a week. The sand is gray with a top layer of glittery, volcanic black. When the tide is out I can walk for miles, picking up shells and watching great flocks of pelicans and frigatebirds. This, coupled with the walks in the jungle around the house, are my favorite things about San Carlos.

Panama has no laws that allow service dogs to accompany the disabled, so Chesty and Rocca are retired from their working lives. Chesty fills his days chasing iguanas and his nights hunting possums. Rocca is still my big-boned shadow. Our family is larger now too. Jack managed to rescue two green-winged macaws, two yellow-headed parrots, and three mono titi monkeys. Will the fun never end?

There are some not so fun things about living here as well. We discovered our first week that while there is a post office in San Carlos, it's only for mailing letters, not receiving mail. Panama has no home delivery system like the one we take for granted in the States. To receive mail is a simple, though expensive, process. We opened an account at Mail Boxes Etc. in the nearby town of Coronado. Sending letters to the States is easy. We just pay three times the cost of stamps in the United States and mail our letters through our accommodating, privately-owned mail service. But sending mail to anyone in Panama is impossible.

Think about what this means. Each and every monthly bill has to be paid by driving to the office of the company providing the service, going inside, and physically giving cash money to the clerk. Seems mildly inconvenient, right? Now, here's how it actually works. We don't get a bill each month for our electricity, water, garbage, phone, internet, or DirecTV. Remember, no home mail delivery system. Actually, this isn't quite true. The electricity bill is delivered by a guy on a scooter who wedges it into our front gate. Most months, we get this bill about two weeks after the due date.

So we receive no bills, but these services have to be paid. Only the water and garbage can be taken care of in San Carlos, and these we pay by the year. Fifty-four dollars a year for garbage and twenty-two dollars for water. We have a septic tank, so that takes care of all the local bills. Electricity, DirecTV, and the internet can be paid in Coronado at the Reyes Supermarket. In theory.

In reality, it usually takes several tries, waiting in line behind twenty or thirty people paying an electric bill of under ten dollars before the computer actually retrieves our account and we can pay our gargantuan $128 electric bill. The only electricity most people use is for lights, and folks that work twelve hours a day don't stay up much in the evenings. The phone bill can be paid in the town of Chame, which is just over twenty-five miles away. Again, in theory. What actually happens is that we drive to Chame and find their hours of operation have been changed, and they're now closed on the day we arrive. Their current hours are Tuesday and Thursday from 1:30 p.m. to 5:00 p.m. Unless they're closed.

The real frustration comes when we have any problems or questions about any of these services, such as when our phone bill showed fifteen calls to Russia and six to South Africa. Here's how that works. We drive an hour and a half to Panama City. Everything is centered out of Panama City. We somehow find the correct office in a city with no street signs. The guard at the door runs a handheld metal detector over Jack and smiles and holds the door for me. Evidently, women are thought incapable of packing weapons.

Now, we take a number and wait our turn. We help ourselves to the free coffee and wait twenty minutes or so until our number is called. We explain our problem to the clerk behind the desk. The clerk directs us to the person handling our type of problem. We take a number and wait. Time passes.

Eventually, our number is called. We explain our situation to a new person, who usually fiddles with a desktop computer, figures out our concern is something he is unable to fix, and directs us to take another number and wait for a specialist. We see our life passing before our eyes and contemplate all the things we had hoped to get done on this trip to the city. Our new number is called, and this person usually fixes it all up for us and sends us on our way to a new number dispenser where we take a number and wait to receive our new, correct bill.

Finally, we have the bill in our hot little hands. We walk with it to a line where we wait to pay the cashier. Once this is done, we bring our receipt back to the person who printed up the bill for us sometime earlier when we were ever so much younger, take yet another number, and wait to have our payment entered into the computer so we can get on with our lives. We've been known to just pay for the damn twenty-dollar call to Somalia rather than go through this procedure.

The second, more significant thing about Panama that I have found to be an obstacle in our relocation is that despite what you see on the internet, the language of this country is Spanish. The only people who speak English are the well-to-do and they live, except on the occasional weekend, in Panama City. In every restaurant, office, store, and hospital, Spanish is the language of communication. As we found out early in this adventure, the only exception to this is on the Caribbean side of the country where most people speak a form of English. In the rest of the country, you must speak Spanish or go without whatever service or item you're attempting to procure. This can be interesting in a restaurant. It's downright dangerous in a hospital.

It's also interesting to live in a country which my country, the United States of America, actually invaded within living memory. During Operation Just Cause, Manuel Noriega was removed and brought back to the United States to stand trial for pissing off the CIA. Panamanian citizens were killed during this invasion.

Panama citizens also celebrate Martyrs' Day. This commemorates an event, less than forty years ago, when American troops opened fire on a group of Panamanian high school students. The ultimate aftermath of this event was the turning over of the canal by President Jimmy Carter to the country of Panama. Each and every time we go to the city, we inch our way along The Avenue of the Martyrs where this happened. This main boulevard is generally lined with anti-America posters.

For the most part, the Panamanian people love Americans while resenting the United States government. Time and time again, people surprise us with their extremely generous and caring natures. Of course, here in San Carlos, we are known throughout the community. Being *gringos* makes us different. Having two huge dogs of a breed that no one has seen makes us interesting. Jack's booming voice, his penchant for practicing his fractured Spanish on everyone he passes, and buying each kid he sees a twenty-five-cent ice cream cone creates entertaining folks to have in town.

All in all, we love living here. I almost never shake and twitch anymore. Really, Jack was right—it wasn't so bad coming down with the two dogs. Everything did turn out just fine. In another ten or twenty years, I'm pretty sure I will have forgotten the whole ordeal. So, if you're looking for a warm, green, friendly, affordable place to retire, come on down.

But bring your trusty pocketknife. Just in case.

www.ingramcontent.com/pod-product-compliance
Lightning Source LLC
Chambersburg PA
CBHW051725260326
41914CB00031B/1742/J